DOWN ON THE BORDER

A WESTERN LAWMAN'S JOURNAL

BY

BART SKELTON

ISBN: 1-4107-8326-X (e-book)
ISBN: 1-4107-8327-8 (Paperback)
ISBN: 1-4107-8328-6 (Dust Jacket)

This book is printed on acid free paper.

1stBooks – rev. 12/05/03

ACKNOWLEDGMENT

These collections of compiled stories takes you through 40 years of life experiences with family, *compas*, and outlaws. 19 years of reminiscing my law enforcement career, the good, bad and the ugly.

I'd like to extend many thanks to my devoted readers, characters I call friends and the acquaintances that I've met along the way that helped to fill the pages and my memories. My thanks for your continued interest in a different way of life, which allows me the privilege to share it through pen and paper.

Thanks to my mother, Sally, and my lovely wife, Kimmie.

This is also dedicated to my friends, family and heroes lost along the way. To Bobby McNellis, of El Paso Saddlery, who passed away on May 11, 2003. *God speed my friend.*

"Like father, like son: Bart and Skeeter Skelton, two of the most talented gun writers ever to pen a thought."

Guns & Ammo Magazine 500th addition. November2001

Table of Contents

INTRODUCTION

To devoted readers and those of you unfamiliar with the published works of Bart Skelton, we'd like to share a selection of his works compiled together in this first edition. These articles have previously been published in *Guns & Ammo Magazine*, owned by *Primedia, Inc.* We selected groups of stories, partnered with illustrations, photos and editorial of friends, that will entertain for years.

Born in Amarillo, Texas, to Sally Jim (Small) and Charles A. *(Skeeter)* Skelton on June 6, 1960, the author grew up in an environment where each of his parents were known in their own right. Many of the stories Bart shares are those of family and icons of that era, in the shooting, hunting and law enforcement arena, as well as *compas* he has journeyed with in his career.

Sally Jim, a World Champion Bull Rider in 1947-48, grew up in the Panhandle of Texas. She appeared in numerous motion pictures during the late 40's & 50's displaying her trick riding skills. She kept company with some of the best loved western movie celebrities of the day, including, *John Wayne, Ben Johnson* and *Chill Wills.* Returning from Hollywood to marry, she continued performing in parades and fairs for her communities for many years. She displays her memorabilia and talks exuberantly about her adventures and opportunities during those early years.

Skeeter, born in Hereford, Texas in 1928, was a U.S. Marine during WWII and spent much of his life in Law Enforcement. Those of you that knew *Skeeter* personally or through his writing, know his legacy will continue in the gun writing world, with his wit, humor and knowledge. As the youngest Sheriff in Texas history, for Deaf Smith County, Texas, his law enforcement career began. He became a mounted agent for the U.S. Border Patrol, went into U.S. Customs, then became a DEA agent in the early 70's. However, he did give a few years to the cattle industry, during the boom years and for 25 years educated and delighted his devoted readers in *"Shooting Times Magazine."*

Bill Leftwich of Fort Davis, Texas, renowned for his art work throughout the world adds his illustrations, marking his take on things Down on the Border. A retired Tank Commander Soldier in WWII, Bill's work had been featured in published works of his own and others, illustrating comical and accurate details. He is a historian and lectures in cowboy hardware, saddles, military history and paraphernalia, as well as the "Wild West" in the Southwest of Texas and Mexico.

Mr. Leftwich's work has adorned U.S. Mint WWII Commemorative coins, he designed the New Mexico Pavilion for the New York Worlds Fair (1964-5), and has numerous acclaims to his life and career. Being able to call him a true friend is an honor.

These selections of Bart's are memories from his childhood through present that depict the life of a famous Gun writers son, a New Mexico State Policeman and Senior Criminal Investigator with the Federal Government.

His stories are visually captivating and will take you to the Southwest desert and cross you over the border, where tough and rowdy men made history, and some still do. Places and events in time that we may never have the opportunity to discover. You will read of firearms used in the past, favorite carries of friends and tales of forgotten and hidden treasures in the expanse of the Chihuahuan and Sonoran deserts.

He illustrates the differences of life on both sides of the Border, as seen through the eyes of men committed to enforcing the law and protecting it. He will introduce you to friends that traveled and caroused with him along the way, teaching him, inspiring him and some that clearly just made his life most humorous.

It's the hope of the author to enlighten you to simple joys of family and friends that we have all shared in life's journeys and remind you to take the time to let them know the joy they bring to your lives. How they and the experiences we share mold our minds, our lives and aspirations.

Things can change quickly down on the Southwest Border, while others always remain. We live just a stones throw away from a completely different, cultural world, filled with wonderful traditions, customs, laws, friends and *outlaws*. So, keep in mind that he and men like him are and have been putting their lives on the line, doing their best to protect our Borders, fighting an endless battle.

Read and enjoy and may his true stories fill your life with laughter and inspire thoughts of what America stands for. Freedom.

FOREWARD

by

H. Joaquin Jackson

H. Joaquin Jackson, Texas Ranger (retired) and Bart showing off
possible trading material, 1st Generation Colt.

The country I'm going to tell you about is some of the most rugged,
hazardous, and most dangerous there is, but still one of the most
beautiful parts of this great land of ours. One of the boundaries of the
border country is the Rio Grande River, known in Mexico as "Rio
Bravo".

The word *bravo,* Spanish for brave, is a good description of this
territory since over the years there have been many acts of *bravizimo*
along her winding banks, which run all the way from El Paso
east/southeast to Brownsville, Texas, a good stretch, indeed.

The lawmen who've worked this part of the country have been just as rugged and dangerous as the land. Author Bart Skelton grew up as one of these type of men under the teachings of his famous father, Charles A. "Skeeter" Skelton. Skeeter too, saw many years of border work as a lawman, serving as a Border Patrolman and U.S. Customs Agent serving in the territory I've described. And not to forget that Skeeter was a hell of a writer. Bart served in the New Mexico State Police, a top law enforcement agency, and is currently a federal investigator stationed in my home town of Alpine, Texas.

Seems the border country has always been the scene of some type of smuggling or other nefarious activity, including the illegal crossing of Candelia wax, bootleg liquor, and now narcotics. Hell, over 50 billion dollars - yes, Billion - flow into this country each year from Mexico, bringing with it a great deal of violence. This is all controlled by the huge drug cartels, who maintain a constant flow of money along with the dope. As a Texas Ranger, I always said a country as big and powerful as the United States could easily stop this nonsense, but I fear it won't happen. I believe stopping this cash flow would throw us into a hell of an upheaval, not to say what it would do to Mexico. And it'll keep happening as long as the *gringos* want the stuff, so where's the solution? I suppose God only knows. But I do know that the officers on the border keep trying, and they've got a tough row ahead. A lot of good men have given their lives trying to stop the flow, and many are still fighting.

So here's to the "Rio Bravo" and the brave officers who continue to patrol her banks.

Now sit back, relax and enjoy a few stories from down on the border, brought to you by a fellow that's been there.

H. Joaquin Jackson, Sgt.,
Texas Rangers, Company "E" (retired)

Section I

CHAPTER 1

Son of a Western Lawman

"Raised under the tutelage of a famous gun writer wasn't always easy, but the author wouldn't have changed a thing."

Dad spoke as he looked out the window of the plane at the expanse of Chihuahuan desert. "Good ol' desert. I do love it so." I could see tears welling up in his eyes, the sight causing an overwhelming feeling of sadness in me. He had just spent the last six weeks in a hospital in Houston, fighting an illness that would defeat him a short time later. I had flown out to pick him up and take him home. As our flight began its descent into El Paso at the eastern edge of the Chihuahuan desert, Dad's relief was immediately apparent.

Though he had been born and raised on the Texas plains, Dad had spent the majority of his life in the Sonoran Desert and the Great Chihuahuan. His first taste of desert life was in the early 1950s, when he and my mother moved to Amado, Arizona, where Dad had been hired by the U.S Border Patrol to work horseback detail in the mountains north of Nogales. Though they took a liking to the place, they also became a little homesick and later headed back to the Texas Panhandle, where he was elected Sheriff of Deaf Smith County. He later became mixed up in the cattle business, did some gun writing and, possibly more taxing yet, wound up with me.

Some might call it influence. Others have described it as wrath. All I know is that Dad's way of thinking about and doing things has affected me in every sense. It began before I could walk. I was assuredly trained on gun safety from the time I could move about unassisted. "No!" was one of the major components of Dad's vocabulary, and believe me, he had no trouble convincing me not to touch a gun, many of which were strewn about the house as indifferently as newspapers might be in other homes. As I grew to more thoroughly appreciate Dad's intimidating, but loving style I was allowed to look at firearms more frequently—with Dad watching intensely. Permission was the essential ingredient in handling a gun and I knew better than not to get it. I never once crossed that line.

I don't remember when it was during my youth that I realized exactly what Dad did for a living. I knew he was a cowman, I later knew he was a policeman, but the writer part of the scheme didn't really strike a chord with me. All I knew was that there were a lot of guns, mostly pistols, around and that we got to do a considerable amount of shooting.

Bart Skelton

I suppose my ignorance as to what went on in his world came through his desire to buffer me, to a certain extent, from the complications and cruelty of real life. Dad's cynicism, a typical symptom in peace officers, was probably a contributing factor. But certainly shooting and hunting were things that he painstakingly taught me. Good ethics and manners, whether we were hunting or shooting, especially with others, were the absolute rule, but enjoyment was always the end result.

When at last I began realizing that Dad was an extremely popular guy with many people besides me, I wasn't really surprised. His readership was immense. I always paid particular attention to Dad's manner when he spoke with a reader or fan he had met for the first time. I was frequently tickled with the fact that, though that person often in awe of him, he treated them just as he would a good friend. When he would take me to the National Rifle Association Convention or other big events, I noticed that many of the "big shots" acted like, well, big shots. Not Dad. Though he would grow tired of the lines of folks waiting to speak with him, he'd never let them see his frustration. He was always willing to listen, to help and mentor people he didn't know. To him they might have been strangers, but most people who admired him thought of him as an old friend, even if they had never laid eyes on him.

After having had dealings with and studying people from virtually every walk of life, I can say with certainty that Dad was on of the last of a dying breed of men. There was not a miniscule portion of his character that was counterfeit, deceitful or dishonest. Unfortunately, we run across such people every day, many of them attempting to copy the characters of men like Dad, thus betraying—instead of carrying on-a fine tradition.

If I could possess only one of my Dad's traits, I would hope it would be his unfaltering character. To say that I was fortunate to have been brought up in such an environment, would be quite inadequate. Dad's knowledge of history, guns and human nature, in addition to his

4

tireless sense of humor, was definitely priceless and treasured by many, and I had the privilege of experiencing it firsthand for a time.

As I drove Dad home from the El Paso airport that last time, he told several stories about various mishaps and adventures he had experienced in the New Mexico desert and it kept me chuckling all the way home. As sick as he was, he never lost his ability to humor and entertain with the truth.

He passed on a short time later, leaving a void for many that will probably not be replaced. Skeeter was better than all of us.

500th Issue of G&A November 2001

CHAPTER 2

The Great Chihuahuan Desert

The border country where I live is without question one of the most remarkable areas in existence and has produced some of the most engaging tales and characters in history. My home is located smack dab in the middle of the Great Chihuahuan Desert which is rivaled by no other, not even the Great Sonoran Desert of saguaro cactus fame. I've spent the majority of my life taking in the treasures of this desert as its student and admirer, and it's a most auspicious place to be.

Growing up just west of the badlands in New Mexico, I was afforded an opportunity that seems to be scarce today. Not a day went by that I wasn't knocking around the brush with a .22 pistol, a good horse and an old dog. These days, my work as a federal lawman along the border prevents me from tarrying in my beloved bush country as much as I'd like, but I still find the time to do a good bit of shooting and consorting with fellow desert rats and to gather alluring tales involving a number of subjects that vary from characters old and new, antics and misdeed of those characters and the accoutrements they have used.

New Mexico's border with the Republic of Mexico commences just west of El Paso, Texas, and runs about 180 miles to Arizona. This stretch of beautiful desolation combines an assortment of desert environments fluctuating from scattered mesquite and greasewood country, through tall grass and pampa to rugged mountain country covered in juniper and pinon pine. All of this area is cattle country, with the exception of a large farming area just west of Columbus, the site of the famous raid by Pancho Villa's revolutionary forces. I can tell you from my personal experience that the New Mexico-Chihuahua border is not much more docile now than it was in the days of the Mexican revolution. It is still a rough and wild country dominated by people tempered by the land, people who make it a habit not to leave the house without some sort of long gun or handgun, depending on the personal taste of the individual. The country necessitates it. I am included in this list and have packed a sidearm almost every day for the past 25 years.

If you look at a map of New Mexico, you notice that the extreme southwest corner of the state bears a resemblance to the heel of a boot, thus the handle "*boot heel*" area. This portion of the state is one of the most uninhabited, wide open frontiers in the United States. I have covered almost every mile of that border fence by one method or other, including helicopter, motor vehicle, horseback and on foot. The lawmen and cowboys who work this country on a daily basis truly have their work cut out for them. The land is ringed by tremendous escarpments that flow into rough, rocky mountain country with little cause for habitation. People, houses and amenities hardly exist. Mexico rambles off to the south and the same variety of terrain is offered there.

This expanse is a mecca for smugglers who thrive on the isolation of the tract. These individuals skulk across the border with their illicit bounty, utilizing every canny method imaginable. For many of these hapless people on the south side of the fence, smuggling is the only way they can scrape out an existence. The introduction of millions of dollars worth of illegal dope into the United States by these folks doesn't always involve sophistication. The *boot heel* area lends itself perfectly to smuggling by pack-train using horses, mules, burros and pedestrians bearing backpacks. Although they are adversaries of our country, I must say that many of the men who ramrod these expeditions are remarkable in their ability to navigate the treacherous

Bart Skelton

terrain mile after mile in the dark of night, avoiding law enforcement patrols that seek them on the ground and in the air. These people are rough, wily and unfortunately, rarely apprehended.

No less hardened are the law enforcement personnel who are tasked with the pursuit of these tough criminal. Rookies sent to the border area to be broken in are done so quickly. If not reared in the area, most eventually come to love the border country for it's harshness and beauty and the strength of character that it had provided them. Equally leathery are the ranchers and cowboys who live off the land along the fence. The border country has fashioned the characters of all of these people.

This part of the country has the essentials for inspiring fascinating tales, many of which have already been composed. For those interested in this type of work, I would recommend Cormac McCarthy's exceptional fiction works, specifically *The Crossing*, which relays an outstanding illustration of the *boot heel* country. McCarthy's old fashioned and striking prose describes the area in detail and captures the reader immediately. His knowledge of this area is unparalleled, as is his ability to describe with certainty his characters, horses and their equipment.

Having been afforded the opportunity to relay some of the stories of my area through this column gives me great satisfaction. Whatever the subject, you can bet that I'll try to talk to you straight from *Down on the Border.*

G&A January 1998

8

CHAPTER 3

The Guides Life

I do get to missing the place. It was one of the most scenic spots I'd ever seen. As a product of the high desert of southern New Mexico, I was immediately captivated by the beauty of the WS Ranch (also known as Vermejo Park), located in the extreme northern section of New Mexico on the Colorado line. I had been lucky enough to land a job as a hired hand bouncing around between several of the ranches work crews.

I was initially hired by the ranch's game biologist, Gary Wolfe, Ph.D., who is now the President/CEO of the Rocky Mountain Elk Foundation. Gary put me to work as one of his assistants; a job offering low wages, long hours and inestimable experiences.

It's well known that Vermejo has one of the most flourishing elk herds in the country thanks to sound management. Part of my job was to haul in bulls that had been killed by pay hunters and help Gary conduct biological studies of the animals. On occasion, Gary also allowed me to hang around with him and some of the guides — an opportunity that gave me considerable insight as to dealing with folks in the habit of paying large sums of money to hunt choice property.

One October day just before one of the bull hunts, two hunters from back east arrived at the ranch. The guides asked that I pick the two up,

9

help get their gear arranged, and take them to the shooting range to sight in their rifles.

At the range, one of the hunters insisted that he needed nothing but cigarette butts for hearing protection. Though I had a couple of sets of *Silencios*, he refused to wear one. Instead he tore the filters off two cigarettes and lodged them in his ears. He then began shooting a nice *Sako* he purchased the day before leaving for the hunt. Firing at a fifty-yard target, he flinched with each shot and generally had a hard time staying on paper. Cussing and clearly having a tough time, Marlboro butts sticking out of his head, he handed the rifle to his partner. His partner, who was wearing good hearing protection, fired several quick shots offhand at the target, with even less luck.

"Better try to shoot that rifle off a rest - I think the scope's no good," he said, handing the rifle back to his buddy. Being the flunky, I decided to keep my mouth shut and just watch.

The first hunter made a few adjustments with his makeshift hearing protection and laid the rifle over the hood of the ranch truck, a brand new Suburban. Without the benefit of any type of rest other than the hood itself, he touched off three rounds in close succession. The shots sounded a little odd, and I figured it was just the echo off the trucks hood. He was shooting at an angle across the hood, standing close to the windshield and firing towards the opposite front corner.

We walked over to the target, discovering that all three shots were a good foot apart. "Good enough for me," he advised. "Let's go ahead and shoot yours."

We walked back to the Suburban where his partner uncased and loaded his new rifle. As he laid it over the hood—and before he shot— we made a frightening discovery: three long, nasty gouges in the hood of the new truck. The first hunter had been able to see the target clearly through his scope, but was unable to see that the muzzle of his rifle wasn't going to clear the top it.

"Ya shot the damn truck you crazy SOB," the second hunter said, laughing uncontrollably. They both then broke into laughter as I tried to figure out how to explain the Suburban's modifications to Gary. As I nervously watched the second hunter fire his rifle, being careful to hold the muzzle high enough off the hood so as not to rip more furrows, I began wondering about the guiding business. I was glad I wasn't taking those boys hunting the next day.

The next morning I headed out to pick up a bull shot by a different hunter and came upon the Suburban occupied by one of the guides and the two hunters from back East. When I paused in the road to say hello and I quickly noticed that their mood wasn't the cheeriest and that the driver's side mirror had been blown off and there was broken glass inside the cab. The guide was fuming.

"What happened?" I asked.

"We came around a curve in the road and ran into a couple of good bulls standing right in front of us," the guide said. "Before I could stop, the muzzle of that rifle was out the window and went off right next to my ear, taking off the mirror and blowing my eardrum. And he missed the bull!"

I then realized that it was the second hunter sitting behind the guide, scowling, while his buddy sat smiling in the front seat with Marlboro butts sticking out of his ears. They were even. Both had taken a piece of the new ranch truck.

Ted Turner now owns what's left of the once mighty Vermejo Park and if he's doing any guiding up there, he's got his work cut out for him.

G&A February 2002

CHAPTER 4

Attacking America, via Columbus

The first time I saw the place I really wasn't too impressed, but a 10-year-old kid rarely can be influenced a great deal by things he doesn't understand. At the time, I suppose, I was much more taken with the immense clumps of lechugilla cactus, the brilliance of large patches of prickly pear in bloom, the decaying walls of the occasional adobe shack and the American flag perched atop the little hill that all of these things surrounded. Since I could see no characteristics that immediately and positively indicated that Pancho Villa had really been there, the remnants of Camp Furlong failed to hold my attention for very long, nor did its host community, the village of Columbus, New Mexico.

Since that time, I have revisited Columbus more times than it would be appropriate to admit. I have stood on that little hill in the middle of Camp Furlong and envisioned how the only true attack on American soil must have unfolded. More times than not during these occasions, the famed actions of U.S. Army 1st Lt. John P. Lucas, the "barefoot gunner," have come to mind. Lt. Lucas commanded the machine gun troop at the 13th Cavalry Regiment, which was stationed at Camp Furlong at the time of the raid.

Francisco Villa and his forces hit the tiny town of Columbus at about 4:30 on the morning of March 9,1916. The exact reason why the

12

bandit elected to pull off such an insufferable act is a point that is still in question, but raid the small village he did, with every intention of slaying every soul possible. Villa's group had formed two separate parties upon crossing the border that lay three miles south of Columbus. The two assemblies made their way through the brush in the darkness and attacked from the west and the south sides.

Having arrived just shortly beforehand on the train from Ft. Bliss, Texas, Lt. Lucas had not been asleep long when the marauders arrived, and he was one of the first soldiers to become aware of what was happening. Hastily pulling on his pants and grabbing his Colt .45 single action, he headed out the door of his quarters and was nearly run down by the mounted Mexican raiders who were yelling and firing at anything that moved. Barely escaping flying lead spat by the raiders' firearms, Lucas sprinted for the quarters of his machine-gun troop. Upon rallying his boys, who were groggily attempting to decipher what was going on, Lucas headed for the shack where the company machine-guns were kept under lock and key.

There were four of them. French, Benet-Mercies, commonly referred to as the "Ben-A." Although light and difficult to handle, they cycled at about 700 rounds a minute, fast enough to help put a dent in the hundreds of attacking Villistas who were mowing down cavalrymen and civilians. But the Ben-A was loathsomely difficult to load and was extremely temperamental in the full-auto mode, often requiring hand-fitting of internal parts by the gunners in order to achieve malfunction-free fire.

Lucas and two of his assistants, one the camp horse shoer, dragged a Ben-A from its storage shed and, under heavy fire, set it up and began firing. To their dismay the gun almost immediately malfunctioned. The gunners then dashed back to the shed and retrieved another Ben-A and without hesitation began firing into the confusion. The horse shoer doing the shooting and Lt. Lucas the loading. Shortly thereafter, the rest of the machine-gun troops joined in with the two remaining arms. A short time after that, numerous riflemen joined in to back up the already hot machine guns.

13

Casualties ran high. The horse shoer was badly wounded but continued to fight. Several of the gunners were hit and some later perished. It was estimated that the Camp Furlong boys, along with the armed citizenry, were firing upon a force of more than a thousand Villistas. Lt. Lucas and his machine-gunners sprayed down the attackers with approximately 20,000 rounds of ammunition in the space of about an hour and a half.

When the Villistas finally began to withdraw, partly due to the casualties suffered from the constant machine gun fire, Lt. Lucas left his troops and headed for the center of the village in an attempt to assist the Villistas' victims. During this escapade, Lucas had the opportunity to dispatch several of the bandits with his .45 single action.

In the end when Villa and his henchmen departed the grisly scene, they left behind close to 100 of their companeros, dead or dying. Horses were dead and wounded throughout the village. Seventeen Americans, among them nine civilians, were left dead.

Members of the 13th Cavalry with Maj. Frank Tompkins in the lead, immediately pursued Villa and his gang to the border fence line and beyond. The troopers shadowed the raiders for the rest of the morning, engaging in several additional skirmishes before returning to Camp Furlong to assist their companions in the bloody cleanup of Columbus.

The following days in Columbus were full of confusion and at times indecision. The following months found the Army led by Gen. "Black Jack" Pershing, leaving the United States for Mexico on a meandering quest of Villa and his crew, which according to some, served only to prepare them for the more distinguished challenge of the Great War.

Today, Columbus, New Mexico, remains much the same as it was before the famous attack—tiny quiet and fascinating, like so many other places that can be found down on the border. And undoubtedly,

I will continue to visit the famous little locale and envision the scene of great American adventure that included Pancho Villa and one of the last exploits of his Great Division of the North.

Guns & Ammo- Oct.1998

CHAPTER 5

Lincoln county Wars

There is a certain atmosphere in New Mexico that is difficult to depict. Generally those who inhabit the place or have spent any significant time there know exactly what I'm referring to. The colors of the landscape— comprised of the softness of various grasses and trees, the shades of geological formations and the unique fashion in which the New Mexico sunlight strikes them all— are major components of the special mood.

Nowhere in New Mexico is that special ambience more pronounced than in Lincoln County, nor have many other counties been the site of such fierce turmoil. Almost anyone who has any interest in the happenings of the Western frontier of the latter 1800s had heard of the Lincoln County Wars and the violence generated from them. Lincoln County was the stomping grounds of William H. Bonney, ("aka Billy the Kid"), Pat Garrett, John Chisum, Dave Rudabaugh and others like them.

Nestled in the mountains of the northern portion of Lincoln county lie the remnants of the village of White Oaks, now referred to as a ghost town, though it is still occupied by various denizens. One of the most bustling communities in the area in the 1800's, White Oaks was, and is, the site of many fascinating -and bloody- escapades.

In the late 1870s, White Oaks sprung up as a boom town virtually overnight after the discovery of a rich vein of gold in the nearby Jicarilla Mountains.

The birth of the new gold town coincided almost perfectly with the initiation of the Lincoln County wars, making it a fashionable hangout for many of the characters of that complex struggle. There have been conflicting stories concerning the demeanor of the population of White Oaks and exactly whose side they took in the matter. It is known that parties of criminal types, several of who reportedly owned trading and rooming houses, reside in or near White Oaks.

Although things often got hot too for the band of criminals in Lincoln or Fort Sumner, White Oaks was in constant need of horses and cattle due to the booming gold mines, making it a great market for livestock. Large groups of criminals held law enforcement in the area in check through intimidation. Eventually, intimidation turned to murder.

In the early days of the Lincoln County strife, White Oaks businessmen Billy Wilson, Tom Cooper, W.W. West and San Dedrick, dissatisfied with profits from legal business, became involved in an elaborate counterfeiting scheme and were soon circulating bad bills throughout the county. It didn't take long for the U.S. government to get wind of the illicit program, and a short time later, undercover U.S. Treasury Agent Azariah F. Wild arrived in Lincoln County.

Through his investigation, Agent Wild was able to identify the source of the fraudulent bills, but ran into a brick wall when he attempted to obtain assistance from local deputy marshals or any other lawmen in the area. It seemed the officers were terrified by the large criminal gangs and wanted no part of Wild's operation. With plans to obtain federal arrest warrants for the counterfeiters, Wild assembled his own gang consisting of Ben Ellis, Franck Stewart, Captain Joseph C. Lea (a wealthy Roswell businessman and friend of John Chisum) and Pat Garrett. The newly formed task force devised an operation they were sure would nail the White Oaks gang.

But before Wild's plan could take effect, the outlaws robbed a U.S mail shipment leaving Lincoln County. Among the parcels were Agent Wild's confidential reports which he had shipped to Washington, D.C. outlining his operational plan. Wild's strategies never materialized, nor did the indictments of the White Oak counterfeit gang, so outlaws continued to terrorize the county.

Around the turn of the century, White Oaks dies almost as suddenly as it had been born. The gold had begun to play out several years before, and many local residents stayed with the notion that the arrival of the railroad through the town was imminent. But greed got the best of the White Oaks citizens who made exorbitant demands on the railroad in an attempt to fill their pockets. As a result, railroad engineers set their sights 10 miles west of White Oak, ending the town's fruitful days for good.

In late 1984, I was sent to Lincoln County as a wet-behind-the -ears New Mexico State Police Officer. My actual duty station was Carrizozo, about 12 miles southwest of White Oaks, which although virtually a ghost town, still carried a reputation of unrest. Several of the locals there continued to feud on a daily basis. One incident involved a prize rooster that strayed to the home of a neighbor and was run over in the driveway. The rooster owner vehemently blamed his neighbor, claiming that the rooster had been assassinated. He then drove his pickup into the neighbors pasture and shot one of his bulls, hooked a chain to the dead bovine and dragged it into the neighbor's driveway. Gunfire ensued, but nobody was hit.

Sometime later, I was dispatched to White Oaks to answer a call involving shots fired. It seemed that two neighbors had become involved in an argument concerning the location of a certain fence line. The defending neighbor was forced to take refuge in his home as the other fired at him with a Ruger Mini-14. My partner and I later counted 180 empty .223 cases fired during the fight. The other man had defended his residence with a .45 Colt Single Action, firing over 30 rounds. Miraculously, on one was hit.

I later watched my partner as he picked up the empty .223 cases strewn about the roadway in front of the .45 shooter's home. He finally stopped and looked around at the beautiful scenery of the Jicarilla Mountains. He scratched his head and turned to me.

"Who says the Lincoln County Wars ended 100 years ago?, he asked.

G&A August 1999

CHAPTER 6

El Paso -Home of the Infamous

Historically, the city of El Paso, Texas, is one the most fascinating places in the United States. By virtue of its geographic location, it has been an important landmark in the annals of the Southwest. Situated on the Rio Grande, which now separates our country from the Republic of Mexico, this hot bed of activity has proliferated for many fruitful—if not bloody—years. As early as about 1530 A.D., people were flourishing at the site of modern-day El Paso, then referred to as El Paso Del Norte (the North Pass), so named by the Spanish adventurers who vanquished the Southwest. For the Spaniards, arrival at the El Paso Del Norte and crossing the Rio del Norte, now known as the Rio Grande, marked the point at which they followed that river north-ward on the famous El Camino Real.

Since those days, El Paso has been the site of countless tales of adventure, peril and mayhem. In the mid 1800s, as gold seekers rushed west-ward to claim their fortunes in the fields of California, El Paso grew even larger as a crossroads. One of the main overland routes from the East found its way to El Paso, and those who arrived with a lot of hard miles ahead opted to winter there, many deciding to stay and partake permanently in excessive gambling, drinking and other lurid deeds. Murder was commonplace. The Mexican government at the time offered bounty on Apache scalps. Some El

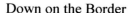

Paso residents took it upon themselves to kill Mexican citizens and sell their scalps as Apache when the Indians were hard to find.

In the later years of the 19th century, El Paso became home to many a famous gunman and others who have been the subjects of extensive study by historians, scribes, lawmen and gun enthusiasts of every type. Among these men are the likes of Pat Garrett, John Wesley Hardin, Dallas Stoudenmire and Jeff Milton. Each of these men and thousands of others like them were perpetually in need of high-quality accessories, generally in the form of long-lasting leather goods. With this in mind, many a saddle maker settled in El Paso, opening his shop to manufacture saddles, bridles, chaps, belts, holsters and other gear to the local users, as well as the many passers-through who would carry the El Paso-made gear to far reaches.

One of the earliest leather-gear makers in El Paso was Frank Andrews, who opened his shop in 1879, catering to the pistoleros of the area. Andrews turned out high-quality leather goods, and it didn't take long for the word to spread. El Paso soon received a reputation for being a hub for fine leather goods, receiving orders from all over the West. Andrews' bustling business later took on other partners, and in 1889, the business became El Paso Saddlery Inc.

El Paso Saddlery was to become a household name in the West among people who used leather goods, especially pistol holster, and that included a goodly number of the characters of the Old West. Garrett, Hardin, Milton, Stoudenmire and famous Texas Ranger Capt. John R. Hughes were important clients and supporters of El Paso Saddlery. But other gunman of the day who were really not associated with El Paso also favored the far west Texas made gear, as was the notorious Butch Cassidy.

Gunman, both honorable and nefarious, were fond of El Paso Saddlery holsters due to their solid manufacture, which resulted form the use of top-quality saddle leather, rather than the thin, softer leather used by other makers. One of the best examples is the two-gun outfit ordered by George Patton, who was stationed at Ft. Bliss, located near

Bart Skelton

El Paso, in the years just prior to world War I. Patton, then a lieutenant, had ordered a Colt Single Action Army (the one he packed into World War II) from Shelton Payne Arms of El Paso. Shelton Payne had purchased the El Paso Saddlery firm in 1902 and offered firearms as well as its leather-goods line. Patton carried his new Colt in an El Paso Saddlery belt and holster outfit on his adventures into Mexico after Pancho Villa and later into the war in Europe. Patton later added a left-side holster for his belt outfit, in which he carried a Government Model .45.

In 1932, the famous saddle maker S.D. Myers purchased El Paso Saddlery and the Shelton Payne Arms Co. and continued to do good business in El Paso for 40 years. Myers used the El Paso Saddlery name for his old-style holsters and harnesses and the S. D. Myers name for the more modern gear, including his beautifully made saddles.

1972, El Paso Saddlery was purchased by Bob McNellis, who is still running strong with the great old leather company. Bob's family has lived in El Paso for more than 100 years. In fact, Bob's uncle, A.A. Howard, was the one-time owner of the notorious Acme Saloon, the El Paso establishment in which John Wesley Hardin was shot down by John Selman. Bob is a notable authority on El Paso history, as well as extremely knowledgeable in the gun trade. McNellis has been an important collector of noteworthy firearms, including handguns owned by Pat Garrett, Billy the Kid and John Wesley Hardin, making him, in my opinion, the ideal man to be supplying today's shooters with some of the finest leather products available. Bob uses the original patterns from the old El Paso Saddlery shop for his old-time holsters. His shop has provided holsters for virtually all of the more recent Western films, including Tombstone, Wyatt Earp, Streets of Laredo and others.

While idling away some time the other day, I stopped in to see Bob at his shop on Yandell Street in El Paso. Bob was seated at his desk, fooling around with an old deck of cards as we chatted.

When I finally inquired from Bob if he was planning on dealing us a hand, he stated "Naw, I just keep these around in my desk. Forgot I had them."

I just looked at Bob in silence.

"They belonged to Pat Garrett, you know," he said.

G&A March 1999

CHAPTER 7

Texas Rangers-Lawmen & Colts

Standing at the very edge of the borderline looking south into the expanse of the Republic of Mexico and all of the enigmas therein, one is mesmerized by the beauty of the mountains in the distance and the history they covet. And whether one might be making these observations from a rickety barbed wire fence looking into Baja California, Sonora or Chihuahua, or the edge of the mighty Rio Grande, peering into the vastness of Coahuila, Nuevo Leon or Tamaulipas, the feeling is much the same. Long before the establishment of the current borderline, when Mexico stretched far into the present day United States, rough men were making attempts to patrol the border on both sides for various reasons and violence was their sustenance.

With the establishment of the world famous Texas Rangers, an end to lawlessness along the Mexican border, or at least a reduction in its cause, was expected. But initially even the Rangers, many times not actually Texans, were sometimes men of questionable background. Often ruffians who volunteered for the job for the sole purpose of being subjected to the opportunity to participate in murderous deeds.

The development of the first successful repeating revolver by Samuel Colt in 1836 was immediately noticed by the Republic of Texas, who became virtually the first customers for the new revolvers. Colt's first shipments of Pattersons to the Republic of Texas initially saw duty on Texas naval vessels. Texas Ranger Captain Jack Hays later acquired a significant number of the repeaters for use by his Frontier Battalion against the Comanche, as well as border skirmishes. During this time, Ranger Captain Sam Walker and his Battalion had experienced tremendous success with Colt's five shot revolver and began corresponding directly with Sam Colt concerning his exploits. Walker advised Colt that the manufacture of the revolver had been a tremendous confidence builder to his rangers and actually had encouraged them to engage enemies who outnumbered them four fold. Walker and Colt later became friends and collaborated on the design of a new revolver of high quality, durability and reliability. The result has been known as the Whitneyville Walker Colt, the Model of 1847 Army Pistol and the USMR Pistol, but is most commonly known as simply the Colt Walker.

The views of the Mexican people in the eyes of the Texas Rangers of the late 1840's was a dim one. Outrageous acts of malevolence was a common occurrence along the border and hatred swelled on both sides. But the Rangers' concern spread into other vehement arenas in the border country. In addition to the constant scuffles with assorted Mexicans, Indian fighting was a very important part of the agenda. Fending off attacks from an assortment of aggressors with black powder armament was an every day task.

As time passed and various wars were seen to an end, the Texas Rangers developed into an organization that sported ranks consisting of higher caliber individuals, dedicated and extremely tough lawmen who have historically held the esteem of people from every walk of life. The escapades of the Rangers along the border country have been epitomized for years and their preference of the Colt Walker revolver and later notorious distinction for their love of the Colt Single Action Army will live forever. Of course there were many other classes of firearms that were extensively used by the Rangers on their escapades, not only in the border country but all over the state of Texas. With the augmentation of the charisma surrounding the Texas Rangers, so increased the quality of their guns and gear.

It seems that the Texas Rangers were invariably first in line to try out the latest developments in firearms manufacture in the line of duty. The turbulent relations with Mexico and the Indians in Texas warranted it. The Henry Repeating Rifle and later the Winchester 1866 "Golden Boy" became trend setters with the rangers, obviously for the same reason the Patterson had. When Colt released its first metallic cartridge revolver in 1873, the Colt Single Action Army, the rangers regaled. The Single Action Army became the official firearm of the Rangers and saw use by the group well after the turn of the century. A short time later, Winchester introduced its '73 Model, an enhancement over the older 1866 in that it utilized a steel frame instead of brass and fired center fire cartridges. Coupled with the Single Action Army, they were an unbeatable pair - equipment that made the exacting jobs of the Texas Rangers easier to deal with.

From the time of the development of the Colt Single Action Army through the turn of the century, the southwest border regions remained a dangerous place for one to hang his hat. The Texas Rangers assisted by various other law enforcement assemblies, continued to enjoy further cultivations of fine firearms. Not all rangers relied solely upon the Colt single action. Neal Coldwell, Ranger in charge of Company "F" in the 1880s, preferred the Colt Model 1877 "Lightning" in .38 caliber, Colt's first double action revolver, coupled with a "Southerner" derringer. Henry H. "Hen" Baker, Texas Ranger and part time Deputy, had an affliction for getting into trouble and was never hesitant about taking a life. His sidearm of preference was the Colt Model 1878 double action .45 "Alaskan" model. In later life, Baker was imprisoned for murder. Captain James B. Gillett fancied a Sharps Carbine in 50-70 to accompany his Colt single action.

Frank Hamer, a famous Texas Ranger who, in the latter part of his career was instrumental in the demise of Bonnie and Clyde, had actually spent a good deal of time on the border engaging various species of bandits. Hamer packed a "C" engraved .45 Colt single action, "Old Lucky", as his primary sidearm and it was said that he was able to shoot it more competently than he could a rifle, and his rifle shooting capability was renowned. In 1922, Remington Arms presented Hamer with a .30 caliber model 8F automatic rifle, heavily engraved with scenes of his flamboyant career. Hamer was also known to favor the 1895 Winchester and the Thompson submachine gun. In an interesting photo taken early in Hamer's career in Del Rio, Texas, Hamer is shown with his Winchester 1894 saddle-ring carbine posed with other rangers in his company, his captain proudly showing off a German Luger. Other rangers were renowned for their liking of the Broom-handle Mauser 9mm.

The Winchester Model of 1894 later replaced other specimens of longarms previously favored by the rangers and other border lawmen, but Winchester's later introduction of the 1895 surpassed even the '94 in popularity and was used extensively by the Texas lawmen through the turn of the century and for many years thereafter. The '94 carbine was preferred for years for its ease of handling on horseback and in automobiles and many lawmen later modified their '95s by shortening the barrel length in order to meet the same criteria.

But the Texas Rangers weren't alone in their partiality towards the Winchester 1895 and Colt revolvers. A few hundred miles to the east, the Arizona Territory was experiencing calamitous troubles with bandits on their border with the Mexican state of Sonora. Shortly after the turn of the century, the governor of the Arizona Territory lashed together a small group of tough cowboys and lawmen and announced them as the Arizona Rangers. Obviously not as long lived or famous as their Texas counterparts, the Arizona Rangers were certainly not lacking in character or the ability to get into and back out of serious forays with various sorts of banditry. Based in Bisbee, Arizona, located just a few miles from the border, the rangers enforced a variety of laws that had previously been ignored by the area's abundant population of smugglers and thieves. Their weapons of choice were much the same as those of the Texans, .45 Colt single actions and Winchester Model 1895s in 30-40 Krag. This combination served the Arizona Rangers well throughout their short but colorful existence.

After the turn of the century, crime continued to oppress the border country in the form of cattle thieves, smugglers and outlaws of virtually every other order. Other forms of lawmen were commissioned to scour the border country, including the Customs Service and the Border Patrol. The individuals hired for these jobs were required to be good with a horse and firearm, have the ability to take care of themselves alone in the border country for extended periods of time and not be leery to enter a skirmish.

In Texas, the federal boys, also armed with the outstanding Colt/Winchester combinations, frequently teamed up with Texas Rangers and even more frequently found themselves in the middle of bad trouble. Not only was the traditional banditry taking place, but repercussions of the Mexican Revolution frequently found their way to the U.S. side.

One particular incident occurred in the Big Bend country of Texas near the village of Pilares, a tough place known for its profusion of banditry. Jack Howard, a well known U.S. Customs mounted inspector (also referred to as "border guards"), was ambushed and killed in the company of two other officers, one a Texas Ranger named Joe Sitter, while escorting a prisoner through the tough Big Bend country. Sitter, who was wounded in the conflict, later became involved in various skirmishes with the assailants and was finally himself murdered in a similar ambush. In recent years, Mounted Inspector Howard' s Colt single action .45 and Customs badge were donated by his family for display at the U.S. Customs Port of Entry at Presidio, Texas.

With the coming of prohibition, conditions on the border failed to improve. The smuggling of illegal booze was epidemic for years and the various agencies who attempted to indulge in anti-smuggling efforts found themselves in jeopardy on a regular basis. Customs, Border Patrol, the Texas Rangers and various other agencies attempted to defend the border with an assortment of armament, some of which are still in use today.

Probably the most widely used sidearm during this time was the Colt Government Model .45 automatic pistol, though many of the old time rangers persevered in packing their .45 Colt single actions. "Old slabsides", as the Government Model is frequently referred to, has seen action in a variety of arenas and has been a standard fixture among law enforcement bureaus since its inception. It is still very common to see a Government Model, Officer's Model or Commander in .45 caliber being carried as a primary sidearm by border law officers.

Known for its reliability and outstanding knockdown power, the Colt .45 automatic is one of the easiest handguns to carry comfortably as the slide is relatively narrow and flat. Officers working in a covert manner can easily slip a Colt .45 in their waistband under their shirt for handy carry, which is a good idea when summer temperatures on the border soar and it's not feasible to wear a jacket.

Since their invention, good double action revolvers have been a favorite among all law enforcement officers, and border cops have been no different. From the old Colt Lightning and Thunderer and Frontier models (1877 and 1878s) through the invention of the swing-out cylinder models perfected by Colt and Smith and Wesson, double action revolvers in an assortment of calibers have made their way into the hands of border lawmen. With few exceptions, agency issued side arms in the 20th century have, until the last few years, been wheel-guns. U.S. Customs investigators commonly were issued the Smith and Wesson Model 66 .357 Magnum for years, which was later replaced by the Smith and Wesson CS-1, a shortened, round butt version of the heavy framed 686 .357 revolver. Both the Model 66 and 686 are outstanding choices for border work as they are durable, reliable and accurate. Smith and Wesson Model 60 .38 Special snub-nosed revolvers are still commonly issued by the Customs Service to their investigators for backup guns.

The U.S. Border Patrol has seen a number of various revolvers as issued side arms since its inception. Though side arms were issued since the onset of the organization, many of the agents preferred to carry their own pistols, generally double action revolvers. After the inception of the Border Patrol in 1924, the standard issue handgun was either the 1917 Smith and Wesson or Colt in .45 Auto Rim caliber, a fine revolver but quiet large in frame, which was combined with issued 1917 Enfield rifles in 30-06 caliber. Years later, old time patrol agent Col. Charles Askins, while assigned as Border Patrol firearms officer in El Paso, Texas, ordered a special shipment of Colt New Service revolvers in .38 Special, which were carried by patrol agents for years. In the late 1950's, Bill Jordan had a hand in the Border Patrol receiving a large shipment of Smith and Wesson Model 19 .357 revolvers which was touchstone for many years.

Today's border lawmen are faced with great dangers in their daily routines as turbulent times continue to prevail on the U.S./Mexico line. With narcotics smuggling at an all time high, defenders of our southern frontier persevere to fight difficult battles, and do so with a diversified assortment of firearms. Many officers and investigators are still carrying single action .45 automatic pistols, but unfortunately many agencies have prohibited their use. The reasoning behind this decision generally states that the single action automatic, with its cocked and locked carrying method, is unsafe and is more susceptible to accidental discharge. This is a decision that many agents, including myself, disagree with.

Through unfamiliarity on the part of the handler, any firearm is prone to accidental discharge. Fortunately for those agents and officers who have been fans of the single action auto, there is a great variety of outstanding autos available. While many agencies require their personnel to carry only the firearms issued to them, several still permit officers to carry an approved personally owned firearm.

Currently, the U.S. Border Patrol and other officers of the U.S. Immigration Service are being issued the Beretta .40 caliber double action only autos. Most of the Border Patrol agents I have spoken with concerning this gun are satisfied with its operation. It has been reliable, easy to handle and relatively accurate. The .40 caliber cartridge seems to be rampant along the border among lawmen and is doing them a fine job.

The Texas Rangers have endured over one hundred sixty years of border conflict and were the first true border lawmen. Their ranks have seen the utilization of an impressive array of guns. Today, about seventy five percent of the Ranger force carry the Sig-Sauer P229 in .357 Sig. The Rangers have been carrying Sig-Sauer pistols for several years with the model P-220 being standard a few years back. Sig-Sauer even offered a Texas Ranger Commemorative P-220 in the early 1990's. Currently, the outfit is extremely impressed with the performance of the .357 Sig caliber. Texas Ranger Johnny Allen of Del Rio, Texas explains that the .357 Sig is deadly accurate, an outstanding man-stopper and probably the most reliable automatic pistol available due to the bottle-neck design of the cartridge which inherently feeds from the magazine to the chamber with ease. The Rangers compliment their Sigs with the Ruger Mini-14 .223.

Unfortunate incidents of lawlessness continue to occur on Mexican border, and it doesn't appear that an end to the conflict is a reality. The individuals assigned to guard our southern boundary will continue to be required to engage antagonists of every type.

So the next time you happen to be down on the border enjoying its beautiful scenery and contemplating its secrets, don't forget to think about those who have strived so to defend it - nor the great guns that have been by their sides.

G&A June 1998

CHAPTER 8

Pancho & Kaiser

"One thing we do very well down here is brew an excellent *cerveza*." said my old friend, Javier, as he tipped an icy bottle of Carta Blanca. I was in total agreement, especially since the temperature outside had exceeded triple digits that summer day in northern Chihuahua, causing an unsightly perspiration stain to slowly spread across the crown of my new straw Resistol.

"The brewing art came to us here form the Germans, you know. Prior to the Revolution" Javier continued proudly.

I had traveled to Puerto Palomas, Chihuahua, that day for a visit with Javier concerning the recent antics of a few of the local degenerates. Javier had been a law officer in the area for some time and was very knowledgeable about such doings. Our conversations would frequently wander to other interesting topics besides who had most recently committed atrocities in the small town of Palomas.

"The Germans infiltrated this part of Mexico during World War I, trying to figure out a ways to get you gringos." Javier informed me.

Germany's interest in Mexico just after the turn of the 20th century-especially in the northern states such as Chihuahua-has been a controversial issue among historians. Indeed, not many people who

32

are interested in the Mexican Revolution days associate Pancho Villa with the Kaiser or any of his minions. But German presence and influence in Mexico during that time is indisputable.

Shady characters have always been drawn to the U.S/Mexican border. Prior to the U.S. entry into the Great War, the Germans provided our southern border with a few nefarious personalities to complicate an already difficult situation. Among them was Felix Sommerfield, a German citizen and world adventurer who had traveled to the U.S., where he joined the Army to fight in the Spanish-American war. Sommerfield later deserted, returned to Germany, and was sent to China during the Boxer Rebellion. Afterward, he made his way back to North American and settled in Mexico, where he became politically active-becoming an ally of then Mexican President Francisco Madero. Before long, Sommerfield was head of Madero's secret service and was responsible for all sorts of mischief on both sides of the border.

After Madero's demise and the seizure of power by Venustiano Carranza, Sommerfield went to work to earn the new President's trust. Carranza later sent Sommerfield to accompany the forces of Pancho Villa and report on Villa's activities. Sommerfield was able to slide right into a position as the main emissary between Villa and influential individuals in the United States, enabling him to become crucial in the purchase of arms from the U.S. by Villa. All the while, he was earning a whopping salary from his efforts.

True to his nature, Sommerfield had no intention of providing any type of loyalty to the Mexican Revolution-or to the American businessmen from whom he was soliciting ammunition, small arms and dynamite for Villa. Sommerfield was reporting on 'villa's activities, no doubt, but no to Carranza as originally planned. His spying efforts were on behalf of the German Secret Service.

Being neutral at the onset of World War I, the United States was providing aid in the form of arms and ammunition to the British, French and other forces-an endeavor that didn't sit well with Germany. Worried that the United States might soon enter the war, the Germans, examined numerous schemes to provoke a major conflict between the U.S. and Mexico that would inevitable halt shipments of supplies to the allies and delay the possibility of the United states engagement in Europe.

The German government attempted to win the alliance of various factions of the Mexican government in many ways. In fact, they attempted to persuade the Mexicans to attack the United States if the Americans entered the war, with the promise that Germany would assist Mexico in recovering the border states of Texas, New Mexico and Arizona.

It is speculated-but not proven-that the Germans were behind Pancho Villa's attach on Columbus, New Mexico, in 1916. It is said that the Germans had promised Villa assistance in his escapades-Sommerfield being right in the middle of things.

Regardless, Germany's effort to charm the Mexicans lasted a long time and required the infiltration of men like Sommerfield who swarmed Mexico for years.

"Beer recipes aren't the only interesting things the Germans left behind, you know," Javier informed me, closely examining the bottle he had just emptied. I looked at Javier questioningly.

"Down southwest of Ojinaga, Chihuahua, some very good friends of mine have a ranch out in the middle of nowhere. The family has lived there for many generations. They have endured many hardships there-and adventures."

Javier went on to explain that the last time he had visited the ranch, he had engaged in a conversation about the old days with the lady of the house, and elderly woman who had lived her entire life on the site. During their visit, the lady had gone to her bedroom and retrieved an old pistol.

"It was a Luger," Javier recalled fondly. "A nice one."

"It had a very long barrel. It also had a shoulder stock, adjustable sights and a large drum magazine. The thing was in excellent condition. No wear at all. It had some nice engraving on the top of the receiver, but I don't remember what it said."

What Javier had described was a Luger P-08 Artillery Model, first adopted by the German Army in July of 1913. It was produced by the Erfurt Arsenal in 1914 and later the Deutsch Waffen und Munizionfabrik (DWM). The drum or "trommel" magazine held 32 rounds and is now a rare find. The piece in it's entirety is one of the most desirable of Luger collectibles.

"How would such a nice gun make it into the hands of a rancher out in the middle of nowhere in Chihuahua?" I asked.

"I don't know, but it's original owner wasn't looking for a new place to brew cerveza, I bet."

G&A September 2000

CHAPTER 9

Geronimo's Apaches

As the desert and mountain regions of the Mexican state of Chihuahua roll northward to the border country and into southern New Mexico, thousands of rugged niches ideal for harboring marauders of all types make themselves available across the land. And until the year 1886, none of this border country was safe from what were known as the "Red Devils", warriors of the various Apache Indian clans that terrorized the souls who inhabited the area. Renowned for their viciousness even today, these people were probably the foremost experts on guerilla warfare that the world has known. Endlessly pursued by the U.S. Cavalry, various militias, vigilantes and bounty hunters, the Apaches were able to move quickly and silently through the labyrinthine border country without detection or apprehension. Most of their pursuers were able to cover 20 to 30 miles per day, but the Apaches were able to travel much farther than that, many times carrying women, children and loot. It is said that Apache warriors were required to have the ability to travel over 60 miles in a day on foot over terrain that would be trying for a mule.

Among the most notorious Apache clans of the latter 1800's was the Chiricahua band, renegades who fled the tedious life of their previous sentencing at the San Carlos reservation in Arizona to continue with their ancient trade of raiding, looting and generally tormenting anyone they could find. Under the capable leadership of Cochise and later Geronimo, the Chiricahua Apaches plundered ranchers, miners, settlers and travelers, their favorite spoils being firearms and horses. Apaches, like most fighting Indians, had a deep love for firearms. It is said that they were probably the most well versed tribe in the use of firearms as they had been trading for them the longest, beginning in the 1500's with the arrival of the Spaniards, led by Coronado.

Amazingly, the Apaches were able to maintain their firearms remarkably well considering the harsh circumstances under which they existed. A good example is the Colt Single Action .45 with belt and holster rig that Geronimo relinquished to General George Crook in September of 1886, the date of the final surrender of the Apaches. The ivory-gripped six-shooter, although sans most of its original nickel finish, was in exceptional condition. The extravagant belt and holster rig, covered with silver conchos and studs hammered out of Mexican coins, was quite worn from extensive employ but nonetheless serving its intended use. The rig was also equipped with a menacing dagger, also in fine condition.

Frustrated in their failed attempts to apprehend the elusive Chiricahuas, the Cavalry turned to the Apaches themselves for assistance. They enlisted members of various other bands who were in exile at the San Carlos reservation as scouts. These individuals, content to escape the regimented boredom of the reservation, jumped at the chance for excitement. They were outfitted with the necessary accouterments, including Trapdoor Springfields in .45-70 Government. Many of these rifles and accompanying ammunition were subsequently traded by the scouts back to the renegades, thus the popularity of these particular rifles with the Chiricahua. Many surviving photographs of the Apache depict warriors yielding the old single shots. Though the scouts enabled the Cavalry to get closer to the renegades than ever before, many were distrustful of them, and rightly so.

Geronimo was an ambivalent man when it came to the reservation. He and his group had been in and out of San Carlos several times, but always seemed to escape and continue with his butchery on both sides of the border. He favored laying up in the mountains of Chihuahua and Sonora, then making large circles into New Mexico and Arizona, leaving carnage in his path. These escapades resulted in the deaths of hundreds of innocent people, women and children included.

While roaming around in this part of the country, it is difficult to imagine the danger that was present during the days of the Apache terror. Going outside of one's home, if not located in the safety of town, to conduct simple chores was a dangerous proposition.

One of my favorite hideouts is the 32,000 acre mountain ranch belonging to my good friend, Mike Laney, which is located near Lake Valley, New Mexico. Lake Valley, now a ghost town, was a booming silver mining camp in the late 1800's and the home of a large company of New Mexico Militia, an assembly well versed in Apache fighting. The Lake Valley area was a favorite locale for raids by Geronimo's band making it an intensely dangerous place for its inhabitants. The homestead of one Brady Pollock, a well known cattleman in the Lake Valley area, was located in the middle of the current Laney Ranch. Pollock's luck ran out in September of 1885 when Geronimo's band, returning from a raiding spree through New Mexico's Black Range, decided to pay the Pollock place a deadly visit.

It was conjectured that Pollock had gone outside of his cabin to milk a cow when the Apaches hit him. Pollock's homestead is surrounded by hills and thickets of juniper and pine, making it an easy spot to keep under surveillance. The Indians brutally murdered Pollock, but not without a fight. There were numerous calibers of empty cartridge casings strewn about the homestead. Mike and I frequently visit the site and have found cartridge casings in various locations about the place, including .44-40s, .45-60s and of course .45-70 Government, which we reckon were fired by Geronimo's men.

Sometimes on quiet evenings I find myself listening carefully to various sounds of calling birds and scanning the brushy areas and skylines for foreign movement, thinking of what it must have been like for the inhabitants of this country over 100 years ago.

The hair on the back of my neck stands on end every now and then.

CHAPTER 10

Black Jack

Passing through the Cofeltt, a large, prickly pear infested pasture on the south end of the Laney Ranch, the road steadily became rougher and rockier as the old four wheel drive pickup bounced southward. The road wound its way through the brushy Cofeltt and up a steep hill, the scenery changing a bit, with pinon and juniper trees dotting the landscape.

At the wheel of the old truck was my brush-beating compadre, Mike Laney, who had worked the rough, southern New Mexico country that was home to his family's ranch nearly all of his life. In addition to being pretty handy with a rope and branding iron, Mike has excellent knowledge of the history of his part of the world, a trait that has held my interest for many years. An avid collector of fine western memorabilia and antique arms, Mike also retains an immense knowledge of undocumented historical events that took place in southern New Mexico in the 19th century. Mike and his family had enjoyed the opportunity to engage in conversations with numerous old-time ranchers in the area had obtained many fascinating tales, some of them first hand.

As we headed down the other side of the steep hill into the Grapevine Spring, Mike pointed eastward into a rough, tree filled canyon containing a natural water flow.

"The tree's right down there in that hollow. Black Jack Ketchum's tree."

I looked intently into the big arroyo, unable to distinguish any one particular tree in the thicket. Mike stopped the pickup, got out and strapped on a Ruger Vaquero .45, his everyday carry gun.

"Let's walk down there and see if we can find it." Mike said as he ambled down the craggy gulch.

As we headed downhill, Mike recounted the tale of Black Jack Ketchum's raid on the railroad north of Deming, New Mexico. Tom E. "Black Jack" Ketchum enjoyed a lengthy criminal career and was famous for making daring raids on trains and stagecoaches throughout the southwest, especially in the four corner states of New Mexico, Arizona, Utah and Colorado. History is a little vague concerning many of Black Jack's forays, but it is known that he ventured into Sierra and Luna Counties in New Mexico and pulled off a few profitable capers. Sometime in 1891 or 1892, Black Jack, possibly accompanied by his brother Sam and other known outlaws, received a tip that the Atchison-Topeka and Santa Fe express train, running a route southbound through the center of New Mexico, was headed for Deming with a sizeable payroll.

Black Jack and his compatriots set up in preparation for a robbery near Nutt, New Mexico, a small water station about twenty miles northeast of Deming. It is believed that Ketchum and his gang had support from some local homesteaders who ran a cow outfit not far from Lake Valley, New Mexico. Ketchum and his boys had used the homesteader's place as a hideout and resting spot and possibly talked them out of fresh mounts from time to time.

The Ketchum gang was comprised of expert train stoppers and the AT & SF to Deming was no match for the seasoned thieves. Just outside of Nutt, Black Jack and his boys stopped the train and ransacked it, discovering the payroll which consisted of about $20,000 in coins.

Being more interested in looting the payroll, the Ketchum gang didn't pay attention to the train's conductor, who ran down the tracks to Nutt and sent a plea for help on the telegraph. A posse was immediately dispatched out of Lake Valley, about 18 miles away.

It didn't take long for the band to figure out that the Lake Valley posse was after them. Good judgment on their part led them back to the safe haven of the homesteaders, a location the Lake Valley posse apparently were unaware of. The posse was never able to apprehend the Ketchum bunch, and Black Jack soon thereafter slipped into Arizona, taking refuge in the town of Clifton. Arizona had no warrants for him and at that time he had not been charged with any federal felonies in that state.

Ketchum continued with his criminal raids for another 10 years. He was apprehended in 1901 after pulling off a robbery near Springer, New Mexico and was hanged in Clayton, shortly thereafter. Those in charge of the hanging were inexperienced and set the rope improperly, resulting in Ketchum's death by decapitation.

The matter of the $20,000 taken from the train near Nutt was never resolved, though many of the ranchers who resided in the Lake Valley area had a good idea what had become of the loot. It seemed that not too long after Ketchum's raid, a family of homesteaders, who seemed to be a little on the shady side anyhow, had pulled up in the middle of the night and left mysteriously. Curious neighbors dropped by the homestead in search of a clue to the family's sudden departure, discovering a large, square shaped hole in the ground, freshly dug. It appeared that the hole had contained a large box. A strongbox, possibly?

"Sometime later, a cowhand rode by and found the map carved into this old tree." Mike said as we continued toward the thicket.

"Word got out that Black Jack camped out here and carved the map into the tree pointing out the location of the money, thinking he'd come back and pick it up later. Some folks said he had done it as a diversion; an attempt to fool the Lake Valley lawmen." Mike said as we walked up on a huge Alligator Juniper tree.

"Did anyone ever follow the map to find out for sure?" I asked, thinking the hole in the ground at the homesteaders place might have been unrelated. Mike grinned, pointing upwards towards the middle of the huge juniper tree.

A flat spot had been sawed off of the surface of the tree about midway up. We could discern some writing, but the majority of the message had been erased by a series of small holes and valleys patterned into the surface of the original map. They looked old.

I looked at Mike in quandary.

"Tree ants." He said with a grin.

G&A October 2000

CHAPTER 11

Ben Lilly

The rugged rim rock country of the Gila National Forest and its surrounding expanse in southern New Mexico is cut by remorseless winds, which can be quite insufferable the majority of the time. The rocky hills are covered with thick mesquite, cholla cactus, cat claw, oak scrub, juniper and pinon, making passage a menacing proposition. The Gila river, small in contrast to many, snakes its way south through the middle of the wilderness and is one of the few water sources, other than the tiny Mimbres, in this tough, dry region. Life is demanding here, but abundant. It is a place where legends have lived and been started.

The favorite retreat of the ruthless Apaches, the birthplace of Billy the Kid and the stomping grounds of Tom Threepersons, the Gila country is the first thing that comes to mind when I think of the Southwest. And while pondering the Gila country, I can't help being reminded of one of its true champions, Ben Lilly. While it is standard for one to think of the true mountain man as an individual lost to the West in the mid-1800s after the collapse of the beaver market, Ben Lilly stands as one of the most famous mountain men of the Southwest, even though he was still alive well into the 20th century.

Born in Alabama in 1856, Lilly grew up a hunter and tracker. He had uncanny strength and endurance and could track for days, even weeks.

He worked his way through the South as a young man, hunting. dealing with horses, trading cattle and farming. He was outstanding with a rifle and a knife—story has it that he killed his first bear armed only with a knife. Lilly chased bear and lion through Louisiana and Texas for years, becoming quite a famous hunter, even guiding Teddy Roosevelt on a lengthy hunt in Louisiana. Lilly later set his sights on southern New Mexico and the Gila country because of the overabundance of black bear, grizzly and mountain lion. He began hunting the Gila country when he was well over 50 years old, remaining here until his expiration.

Ben Lilly killed an implausible number of lion, black bear and grizzly in the rough country of southern New Mexico, eastern Arizona and south of the border. He allegedly killed six bear and four lions the first week he arrived in eastern Arizona. It is said that he averaged about 50 lion and bear per year and made good bounty money. If Lilly was informed of the attendance of lion or bear in a vicinity, he and his large pack of dogs tracked it down easily when most so-called professionals were unable to catch a glimpse of the animal. He also became a skilled naturalist, providing specimens of many of his kills to museums, universities and to various biologists. Lilly had no fear of his prey. He considered it no feat to finish a wounded grizzly bear with his hunting knife. On one particular occasion, Lilly tracked a wounded grizzly in deep snow and was later charged by the beast. He fired several shots into the bear and finally finished it by plunging his knife into the animal's heart. This bear measured nine feet from nose to tail and eight feet in girth. The skull and hide were sent to the U.S. Biological Survey in Washington, D.C., for which Lilly did a good deal of work.

I've been blessed to have had the opportunity to have known a number of fascinating people, among them the late Laurence Laney who ranched and outfitted to the Gila country for more than 70 years. I recall passing evenings with Laney and his son Mike at the Laney ranch near Lake Valley. Laney had vivid memories of Ben Lilly, who had frequented the Laney's ranch, in eastern Arizona in the early 1900s. Laney's father, Will, ranched near Clifton Arizona, and came to know Ben Lilly well. In 1918, Lilly contracted pneumonia and stayed with the Laneys for months while recuperating. Even while deathly ill, Lilly refused to sleep in a bed, preferring to lie on piled-up clothes on the ground or on the floor and spending very little time in the house.

Laurence stated that Lilly hunted and tracked bear and lion for days with his dogs and would seek out small holes in the ground or tiny rock caves, crawl into them and sleep comfortably. During the daylight hours, while tracking or traveling, Lilly would hike for miles, wearing out double-soled footgear in no time.

Lilly would return to the Laney place on occasion for short visits in between lengthy bear- and lion-tracking sessions into Mexico and along the border country. On one of his last visits, Laurence recalled, the old man Lilly, memory slipping, was on a quest to find his newly purchased Winchester rifle. It seems that Lilly had headed into Silver City, New Mexico, to Cosgrove's Hardware store and purchased a new Model 1894 30-30 after hearing that the company would soon discontinue the longer-barreled gun and only offer the shorter carbine. Being a thrifty man, Lilly decided that since he had not completely worn out his old rifle, he would hide the new one in a cave in the midst of the Gila until he needed it. Of course, he forgot the exact location of his stash site.

Ben Lilly is a great part of history, especially in the Gila country, but unfortunately I often find that many people are unaware of his story these days. Thankfully, Ben Lilly was immortalized by the great writer J. Frank Dobie in his book *The Ben Lilly Legend*, which is must reading for all hunters.

If you happen to be ranging in the Gila country, let no cave go uninspected. There's a good chance Ben Lilly's lost Winchester may be looking for a new home.

G&A June 1999

Section II

- Bill -

CHAPTER 12

Pure Guts of a Ruger and Chapo

The summertime heat down on the border in southern New Mexico often becomes intolerable to the point that folks occasionally find themselves doing things they otherwise might not. Many who make their livings out-of-doors are especially vulnerable to precarious mood swings and other irritable types of behavior during the sweltering southwest summer. One of the worst parts of this scenario is the duration of the southwest summers, which seem to roast the land and its inhabitants for months.

It was just such a summer a few years back that found me conducting a torture test on a Ruger Redhawk .44 Magnum revolver. The test involved firing thousands of rounds of full house .44 Mag through the gun in order to test its durability and accuracy after extended use. Many might consider this chore to be somewhat demented, not only because it's common knowledge that the Redhawk is virtually indestructible, but subjecting oneself to shooting that much full house .44 at one time, may, to some, seem a little questionable. My friend, Will Schmitz, and I conducted the test over a period of several weeks, shooting 1000-1500 rounds per session. Call me fastidious, but after each of these sessions, my nerves tended to stay on edge for several hours afterward.

The one consolation at the end of the harrowing shooting sessions was the fact that my favorite watering hole, the Adobe Deli Saloon and Steak House, was but a few miles away from the chosen shooting site. One evening, after a particularly hot and jolting session with the Ruger, I decided to stop in and say hello to my friend and owner of the Adobe Deli, Van Jacobsen.

Van's fine establishment is a haunt for all types of border characters, including cowboys, bankers and cops. It is generally quiet and sports a friendly atmosphere, but this evening was to be somewhat out of the ordinary.

It was nothing new that a few of Van's clientele had over-indulged a bit, most likely a little carried away in trying to cool off from the intensely hot day. But one of the regulars, 'Ol Chapo, seemed to have gone just a bit too far. Chapo was a cowhand employed by one of the area's big ranches. Small in stature, the cowboy had been around a few years and had the tough appearance, and scars, to prove it. He had ridden bad horses all of his life and worked at just about every big ranch in the western states, or so he claimed. Chapo often had a bad disposition to go along with his powerful propensity to imbibe Van's cool libations.

That evening, Chapo had experienced the misfortune of seeing the better portion of his meager paycheck find its way into Van's cash register. Thirst then overpowered common sense, and Chapo found himself keeping a close eye on Van, waiting for him to leave the bar long enough to re-hydrate. Van generally kept a tray underneath the beer taps to capture overflow, having to empty it once an hour or so. Van apparently hadn't noticed that it had remained empty much longer than usual. During my conversation with various patrons, I caught a glimpse of Chapo dashing behind the bar and swilling the stale, flat beer from the tray. Several flies had collapsed into the brew and were also downed.

Having a soft spot for cowhands down on their luck, I invited Chapo over and offered to buy him a cool one, which he accepted. Not being satisfied with the initial offer, Chapo later insisted on wagering money on various topics, most of which consisted of stunts not acceptable in the general public. I declined Chapo's bets and attempted to mind my own business, which further aggravated the situation.

"I'll bet you five dollars I can sniff this Copenhagen snuff right up my nose." Chapo exclaimed.

Several of the saloon constituency briefly looked up when the statement was made, but quickly returned to what they were doing. I attempted to ignore the wager.

Shortly thereafter, Chapo was pouring a nice sized portion of snuff onto his hand and forefinger. His eyes then flickered across the bar and his gaze quickly affixed itself to a bottle of Tabasco pepper sauce. Liberal doses of the sauce were then deposited across the snuff. In one mighty induction, air, snuff and Tabasco were vacuumed into Chapo's nasal passages.

When the sneezing, coughing and arm flailing was finally over, Chapo unbelievably re-claimed his seat on the bar and resumed downing his beer, peering at a heavy, genuine rock glass which was perched on the bar in front of him. He looked at me with a steely eyed stare.

"Twenty bucks says I can eat that glass."

Before I could respond, Chapo grabbed the glass and bit a large chunk out of it. I sat in disbelief, wishing I was back out at the range with the Ruger. Chapo actually chewed the broken glass, which sounded like large pieces of ice being chomped by a youngster. He then turned to me with a grin that was somehow amusing, blood running down his shirt.

Before I knew it, Chapo grabbed my shirt collar and kissed me squarely on the cheek, afterward letting out a chilling yell. Brushing off blood and broken glass, I was unable to decide whether to clobber Chapo or break out laughing.

Before either could take place, Van was escorting Chapo out the front door, the wild-eyed cowhand demanding his twenty dollars.

A few days later I was back at my post, firing round after round of .44 through the Redhawk. The heat was stifling. My nerves were on edge. I thought of refreshment at Van's place just down the road. I then thought of Chapo and the fact that he had endured another hot day of working cows and had no doubt developed a powerful thirst.

It then occurred to me that Van and I needed to work on landing Chapo a new job. Computer sales? Stock broker?

Anything indoors.

G&A April 2000

CHAPTER 13

Pocket Pistols

Pocket pistols have always brought out a good deal of curiosity in me. The notion of a small, concealable, easy-to-handle handgun is quite appealing for a variety of chores. Even though I am fond of the big .44s and .45s, I rarely venture far from one of my little pocket guns. For many cops, the thought of being without a backup gun is completely unthinkable. And with the popularity of concealed carry on the rise, pocket pistols have a firm place in today's handgun world.

Pocket guns have been in use for many years and first emerged in the form of short, single-shot and sometimes double-barreled flintlock and cap-and-ball handguns. In the early years of percussion-cap revolvers, Colt produced the New Pocket, the New Model Police, the New Model Army and the New Model Navy—all very lightweight five-and six-shot, .31- and .36-caliber revolvers made to be easily concealed and carried. Literally hundreds of thousands of these little guns were manufactured by Colt between 1849 and 1872, indicating the vast popularity of that particular size of firearm. In 1870, Colt began expanding its line of small pistols, including the Number One Derringer, a single-shot .41 Rimfire. Colt later continued its production of small guns with the House Pistol and New Lines, sometimes known as "Cop and Thugs," which were other variations of pocket guns. Colt's success with small firearms continued with the introduction of the Colt Model 1877 Lightning and Thunderers, the company's first double-action revolvers and my own personal favorites in the antique Colt lineup. Even the ever prevalent Single Action Army was brought into the swing of the pocket gun by Colt with the Sheriff's Model variation, which sported a short barrel and no ejector rod or housing. The Sheriff's Model was a quick, light belly gun available in a variety of calibers. Today, a first generation Sheriff's Model is an extremely desirable item among collectors and would bring a premium price.

But Colt certainly wasn't the only gun manufacturer exploiting the popularity of small handguns in those days. The market in the 1800s was flooded with small European-manufactured pistols, such as the Belgian and French pinfires. U.S.-made solid-and hinged-frame revolvers in a variety of calibers were manufactured by a large assortment of makers. A classification of small, single-action revolvers known as Suicide Specials were extremely fashionable. These little revolvers were of solid frame with spur triggers and cylinders that were freed by the extraction of a center pin. Although the number of manufacturers of the Suicide Special were myriad, some of the more prevalent were Hopkins & Allen, Forehand & Wadsworth, Bacon and Iver Johnson. These guns were small, cheap, easily obtained and very much relied upon by the masses until about 1890. They were available in virtually every type of emporium imaginable and were very popular mail-order items, varying in price from 60 cents up to several dollars each. At these prices, virtually everyone owned a Suicide Special, and some carried two or three. But as law enforcement presence increased, the hey-day of lawlessness dwindled along with the Suicide Special. Mass productions of the small revolvers remained boxed in factory warehouses for years.

After the turn of the century, the production of high-quality pocket guns continued and subsisted beautifully. Colt produced a series of fine automatic pistols in the early 1900s that included .32 and .38 Rimless Pocket Models and a tiny .25 Auto Pocket Model, all hammerless in later years. Colt introduced its famous snub-nosed Detective Special, along with the Baker's Special and the Pocket Positive revolvers, which were available in .22 Long Rifle, .32 Colt,

Bart Skelton

.32 Smith & Wesson and .38 Special. The Colt Cobra with its light, alloy frame was also a fine snubby.

Right alongside Colt on the list of fine pocket guns has been Smith & Wesson with its excellent little Centennial and Chief's Special short-barrel .38 revolvers. These guns were, and still are, ideal hide-out pistols. I currently own a Smith & Wesson .22 caliber Kit Gun, a small, two-inch revolver with adjustable sights that is ideal for carrying in a day pack, tackle box or any other carry bag. It is light but extremely accurate and a real pleasure to shoot. I wouldn't recommend it as a hideout gun for police work, but it's great for a camp gun and certainly would suffice for self-defense if nothing else was available.

These days, excellent pocket guns abound. Small pistols that have typically been used by law officers as backup guns are now looked upon as ideal carry guns for those with concealed-carry permits. Little pistols that pack a heavy hit seem to be the order, and there are numerous auto pistols available in .45 Auto that are incredibly small yet do their jobs in fine fashion, the Glock being a prime example. And it seems that many pistol manufacturers are concentrating on lighter, sleeker, heavy-caliber pistols, a practice that I certainly agree with.

As for me, I mostly rely on my Walther PPK/S in .380 as my everyday pocket gun. As a New Mexico state police officer, I began packing the little .380 neatly tucked in my Sam Brown rig where it was comfortable, unnoticeable and easily accessed. I later started carrying the Walther as a backup at the beginning of my career as a federal officer. The little 380 is very well-worn, and I rely on it daily. It is with me off-duty as well as on, and I rarely leave the house without it, as it is extremely light and handy.

Things can occasionally get ugly down in the border country where I live. When the chips are down, it never hurts to have a little backup. You can bet that I'll have an ace in the hole.

G&A November 1998

CHAPTER 14

My boots or him?

For many years, footgear of exceptional quality and perfect fit has been a must for those hearty individuals scraping out a living along the border. Cowmen, lawmen and many other border types have long been known to dole out a month's worth or more of hard-earned wages on a good pair of boots. Solid protection of the feet along with comfort are a must in the spiny, rock-laden terrain that exists along the majority of the border country. Like a good rifle or sidearm, a fine pair of *botas* is an essential part of the border person's gear, and I know many who don't blink at the prices good boot-makers command.

Many of my border *compañeros* and I prefer the superb products offered by the Paul Bond Boot Co. of Nogales, Arizona. Paul has been in business for many years and is well known for his long-lasting, hard-wearing, made-to-measure boots. Although pricey, they fit like a glove and last through years of hard wear under difficult conditions— the same attributes, actually, of a good firearm. Many are initially reluctant to shell out the price of a pair of Paul Bond's, but once they actually have them on their feet, they are rarely disappointed and usually cherish the finely made boots.

A few years back, I happened to be cooling off at a watering hole near Mesilla, New Mexico, when I ran into a fellow border agent whom I hadn't seen in ages. He was sitting quietly alone at a corner table watching the clientele, his back against the wall, and sipping a cold beer. He waved me on over, and of course, I immediately joined him. Having been retired for a few years from his border lawman work, the weathered old border rat was looking a little rough around the edges, but he had seen years of difficult times on the border, including scrapes with border criminals of every type. He had been a cowhand and horse breaker in his younger days before taking a job as a border agent. He was dressed, as always, in a sweat-stained silver belly hat, khaki shirt, S. D. Myers pants belt with a fancy four-piece ranger buckle, Levi's and a pair of sharp-looking Paul Bond boots with high, under-slung riding heels. No doubt his attire included a belly gun of some sort, but he kept it well concealed. He actually looked more like an old cow buyer than a cop, and he was well-versed in the dealings of the cattle trade, although it wasn't his main concern. The old reprobate had introduced me to Paul Bond years before, and I had become a fan of the boots myself as a result.

Our conversation that afternoon wound its way through a variety of subjects, including the state of law enforcement agencies enforcing drug laws along the border, at which time the old man did not hesitate to express his opinion, which—to put it lightly—indicated that the various agencies had taken a spiraling nosedive into the true depths of failure. He said that the old days of true law enforcement were gone for good and that the age of computers and liberal methods of carrying out the law had forever changed things and that conditions would only get worse. He indicated that the big drug cartels and organized crime had won long ago and that nobody really cared about it anymore.

As the conversation eased up some, the older man enlightened me with stories detailing a few of his more delicate escapades on the border. One entailed the ill enterprises of an old smuggler known as "La Liebre," the jackrabbit. La Liebre had come from a well-known family of marijuana smugglers from down around Delicias, Chihuahua, and was renowned for his uncanny ability to evade the police, having done so in just about every type of pursuit conceivable. He bragged about his dope-running ability and about the fact that he could never be caught. But my old friend had ferreted out a relatively reliable informant who had been keeping him apprised of La Liebre's smuggling activities.

The old-timer looked at me over his beer with a cold look in his eye. "My snitch was an old smuggler, too. Lived down around Delicias near La Liebre's place. It seemed that La Liebre had set up a few of my informant's runners and stolen about 300 pounds of his weed. The old guy was about half afraid of La Liebre and figured the best way to get even with him was to get him busted on this side, so he came to me. He found out that La Liebre was fixin' to do a deal on the U.S. side [of the border] near La Union, just upriver from El Paso. Supposed to have been a big load of grass. Knew exactly when and where the deal was to take place. I slipped down there and hid my car out in the brush near a big irrigation ditch full of water. Sure enough, just before sundown, La Liebre showed up at an old abandoned horse ranch and met with a couple of fellows in a bobtail truck. When I saw them open up the back of the truck and show off all those big packages of dope, I jumped on out there with my Government Model drawn. The two boys that had been in the truck froze, and I got them taken care of easy enough, but sure enough, that damned La Liebre took off runnin'. He hit that big irrigation ditch, swam it and ran off through the brush on the other side. I had just gotten a new pair of Paul Bond boots and was just beginning to break them in. Sure hated to jump in that ditch an' ruin 'em. I looked down at them boots, looked at the water and then at that damned smuggler gettin' away again."

The old gent looked away, took a long pull on his beer and then lit a cigarette. He sat there smoking, shaking his head.

"So he got away again?" I asked.

"Hell no." the old cop said. "I just shot him".

G&A December 1998

CHAPTER 15

Gate's .357

Springtime in the extreme southwest sector of southern New Mexico kicks up strong winds resulting in momentous dust storms, a product of the desert's lack of vegetation. Temperatures during this time are just beginning to rise, causing inhabitants to sweat just enough for the blowing dust to spackle faces and necks, the aftermath ranging from maximum discomfort to general misery.

It was just such a day a few years ago that my fellow drug agent, Tommy Bowles, and I were conducting an anti-smuggling operation in the New Mexico boot heel when distress and thirst overcame us. The boot heel area of New Mexico is a tremendous expanse, and watering holes are few and far between. Located more or less in the middle of this tract is the old mining camp of Hachita, a small village sporting numerous old adobe houses, a gas station and cantina. Tommy and I subjected ourselves to frequent stops at the Hachita cantina, not only because of the fact that the cold drinks were great remedy for dust parched throats, but also for exposure to the establishment's clientele, which ranged from local mine workers, a few smugglers, ranchers and cowhands, all of whom could usually provide interesting insight of some sort.

Border drug agents, believe it or not, are not always welcome in border cantinas. This particular day was par for Tommy and I. After ordering cool drinks, our attention became fixed on a gentleman seated at the end of the bar who was hurling insults in our direction with the rapid fire call of an auctioneer. He was a tall, lanky sort with a very large mustache, pants tucked into his high-topped boots, fancy Garcia spurs and a hat so foul that it appeared to have been drug through the inside of a mule. Tommy attempted to calm the cowhand with verbal judo, however failed, and we continued to sip our refreshments while enduring the barrage. We then bought another round, including one for the salty cowhand, a gesture that seemed to calm him somewhat.

After imbibing a few cool ones on us, the old hand, who ultimately distinguished himself as Roy Gates, eased up on the surliness and began addressing us in a more merciful tone. Tommy and I gleaned that Roy was in the employ of a large ranch that regulated many miles of Mexican border country. Upon the completion of several more libations, Roy related to us various tales of his tribulations along the border which included troubles with drug-smugglers, cattle thieves and ruffians of assorted stripe. I asked Roy if he frequented the border fence country unarmed, and received a caustic, negative reply. Roy advised us that he rarely ventured away from the house without his .357 revolver.

As the hour became later, Tommy and I elected to make our way back to civilization for the evening, declining Roy's offer for us to make the 35- mile trek down to his place near the border to stay the night.

Some time later, Tommy and I found ourselves detailed back into the boot heel on a similar operation that led us into the vicinity of Roy's place. Recalling the remoteness of Roy's home and that he had mentioned that he rarely ventured to town, we picked up several cases of beer, a carton of cigarettes and several boxes of .357 ammo for the cowboy. Following directions previously provided by Roy, Tommy and I guided our truck down miles of rough dirt road toward the house, hindered by the blowing dust brought upon us by the spring gales. Our arrival at the ranch house found Roy unsaddling a rough looking old horse. He was dressed exactly the same as he had been the evening we had met him, with the addition of a coarse looking pair of chaps and a mighty revolver contained in a worn out Kirkpatrick belt and holster that was strapped outside of the worn leggings.

Unsmiling, Roy approached us, cigarette protruding from under his immense mustache. He gave us a hard look, then offered his hand. Greetings were exchanged and our gifts provided. Upon receiving the .357 ammo, Roy exclaimed that he appreciated the thought, but they were the wrong caliber. Drawing the eight inch hand cannon, Roy advised that his .357 was more powerful than just a regular Magnum. I immediately recognized the revolver as a Dan Wesson .357 Maximum. Roy counseled that it was the ideal caliber for brush country work.

Roy invited us inside for a cold drink. Roy sat us down and advised us that several pack trains of mules and horses laden with drugs had crossed the border fence in a remote pasture in recent days, cutting the fence and traveling north bound. We mapped out plans to saddle a few horses and track down the offenders.

Mid afternoon found us horseback in beautiful desert mountain country along the New Mexico/Chihuahua fence line. After discovering the precise location of the intrusion by the contraband-laden pack train, we headed north in a meandering pursuit that would later turn out to be fruitless. As we rode, Roy told me that he had been a cowhand for more than 20 years. He said that seclusion from the atrocities of today's world were well worth the near poverty-level income that he endured. He said that his salary was just enough and that any more would cause him to venture to town more often, which he'd just as soon not have to do.

That night on the way back to town, Tommy reminded me that it was necessary for us to immediately complete all of the paperwork regarding our little operation. He also reminded me that we were way behind on our regular reports since we had been in the field for several days instead of in the office. Our vehicle reports, daily reports, monthly reports and supply reports were overdue. The radio dispatcher called and advised our supervisor had been unhappily looking for us for hours. I recalled the stack of unpaid bills laying on my coffee table.

I pondered on Roy, his tremendous .357 Max and his anxiety-free style. I wondered if the ranch was hiring.

G&A June 1998

CHAPTER 16

Spanish Antiquities

Antique Southwest artifacts, particularly firearms, are rapidly becoming an evaporating commodity in this world, at least for the shallow-pocketed fanciers of such things. Collectors from every corner have sallied northern Mexico and its bordering U.S. states over the years in search of antiquated prizes. Most of the good guns, especially old Colts and Winchesters, have long since been commandeered by pawnshop men and other hoarders. Equally valuable are other Old West memorabilia such as leather gear, whiskey decanters, various gambling instruments, saloon tokens and more. But these, too, have fallen prey to the big city antique amasser looking to make a buck on the surviving articles of days gone by.

Even more difficult to come across are relics of the Spanish exploration. Now and again, one might find an old Spanish spur or stirrup, but armor and other valuable mementos are scarcely found, though thousands of Spanish adventurers once roamed the Southwest.

One hot, dusty spring day a few years ago found me passing time in an obscure little watering hole near Lewis Flats, New Mexico. The Adobe Deli Saloon, run by an old amigo of mine named Van Jacobsen, has always been a gathering place for border rats looking to cool off from a hot day of ranching, farming, vagrancy or whatever. The Adobe Deli has been the blame for my encountering a number of curious border characters, some a little on the salty side, but nonetheless interesting. This day found me in the company of one of the most interesting of my Adobe Deli acquaintances, a gentleman who had moved to the Southwest after growing tired of the stringent gun laws. A retired engineer, my friend had come to southern New Mexico from Australia seeking work as a cowhand and had found plenty of it. When not working cattle, he busied himself building guns and unique accessories for them. and also exploring various sectors of southern New Mexico that he had heard about during his days Down Under.

As my Aussie friend sat washing down New Mexico dust with one of Van's ice-cold libations, a variety of topics weaved their way through our conversation, including the subject of dug-up antique guns and other commodities that could be occasionally dug up in the right locale.

After some time, my *compañero* glared at me with a solemn gaze, pulled his hat down over his eyes and looked around the bar, checking for eavesdroppers. He motioned me closer, asking me how well I knew the Florida Range, the stretch of rugged, unforgiving mountains that stretch from just north of Columbus, New Mexico to a spot just west of Lewis Flats. I replied that I had been raised in that country and had been stomping around the Florida Range (pronounced flor-ee-da, so named by the Spaniards who were impressed with the yearly growth of poppies in the area) almost all my life.

My friend took a sip from his icy glass and explained that he had recently been on a horseback trip on the southwest end of the Floridas when he and another companion made an exemplary find. He and his cohort had been riding through a particularly rough series of canyons when they happened to stop for refreshment. While scanning a brushy area below them, they noticed an object— definitely man-made— protruding from between a large granite boulder and an old, weathered juniper tree. Their examination of the object resulted in a feeling described by my friend as the sensation one must experience after hitting the lottery.

Bart Skelton

"It was a cannon," he said.

I looked at him quizzically.

"It's made of brass, very old. Brought over by the bloody Spaniards. It's burst open in the middle and they tried to repair it by wrapping the ruptured part in wire. It's huge, too," he said. Though I was a little taken back by my friend's statement, I wasn't necessarily surprised. It coincided with stories I had heard for some time about an abandoned Spanish cannon in the Floridas. A great archeological prize.

"But how could it have gotten there, of all places?" I asked. "The Apaches," he said. He went on to explain that it had been a common practice of the Apaches to haul booty they had seized from the white man into remote areas and destroy it. It is known that Apaches had taken cast-iron stoves, wagons and other articles they had seized into the hills and broken them into small pieces, condemning every aspect of the white man's advance.

We then began to lay plans of rediscovering the site. My friend told me that the cannon lay wedged between the rock and juniper and that the tree had grown over the top of it, making it virtually impossible to dislodge without tools. We made plans to pack in a good chain saw and crow bars, and a strong rope would be needed for the horses to drag the old artillery piece out.

During the planning, I could see in my would-be partner's eyes that a problem persisted. "I can't find it again, mate. I've been back two or three times and I just can't find the same canyon. All of those little canyons look the same." His head hung sorrowfully.

My meanderings through the unforgiving slopes of the Florida mountains since then have been full of hope that I, too, might get a chance to see the weathered old Spanish cannon, but to no avail. The desert growth has hidden it well. But even without rediscovering the old piece of ordnance, just being in the desert and mountains,

64

enjoying the panorama without having to deal with the tensions of modern life, knowing that there is a possibility that the cannon might again show itself, is a great feeling.

Sometimes I think the Apaches had the right idea.

G&A July 1999

CHAPTER 17

Hamilton and John, If only I had..

"Look out for the ol' boy who's only got one gun 'cuz chances are he really knows how to use it."

It's an aphorism that has been repeated for years and holds true no matter how it is said. There are archives of material available on the subject, and most "If I only had one gun" pieces make for enticing reading as each writer expresses his convictions of various divisions of firearms and the all-around practicality of their calibers. It's also a subject that doesn't sit well with many firearms enthusiasts because they can't bear the thought of having only one gun, speculating that this situation could someday present itself as a result of dire financial or political times.

When it comes to the "only one" handgun issue, hackles ruffle, dust flies and donnybrooks flourish. The question of "Double-action revolver or auto pistol?" is recurrent among lawmen, and the debate over single action vs. double action among hunters and plinkers is perpetual. But considering the quality of every conceivable configuration of guns available these days, the "which is best" point is hardly arguable, nor is the element of someone's personal taste, which is not something that should be disparaged whether it regards guns or any other subject. This all absolutely boils down to the fact that the shooter should work with the firearm that he or she is the most comfortable with and shoots most proficiently. This is true whether you're carrying a sidearm as a law officer or a handgun hunter or you simply keep a handgun around for personal protection.

I frequently muse on the one-gun theory, and I must say that, like every other devotee, I find it to be a tough choice. Complicated, enduring and fascinating devices, firearms should also be considered works of art. Accurate, well-tuned revolvers and automatics can be greatly enhanced by fine finishes and fancy, well-fitting stocks, making for a completely satisfying and utilitarian tool. Were I faced today with the burden of choosing a one and only sidearm, I would turn to one of our many customizers of fine firearms to be certain that my gun was exceptional. Fortunately, there are numerous individuals actively in the business of hand-tailoring some of the finest firearms that have ever been available.

If a single-action revolver turned out to be the preference, we are lucky enough to have several fine pistol smiths available to detail a good gun to one's exact specifications. Bob Baer of Rosenburg, Texas, has accomplished some of the most interesting work I've seen on Ruger single actions. Bob's work includes re-shaping grip frames to the measure of the shooter's hand and fine custom barrel work, including octagon and tapered barrels, superb finishes and some of the best action work I've seen. I've shot many of Bob's guns, and they are all exceptionally accurate.

Another fine single-action customizer is John Gallagher of Jasper, Alabama, who is performing extraordinary work on Rugers. John has been building conversion guns in several calibers including the .445 Super Mag, which I have found to be an outstanding choice for anyone interested in big-bore shooting.

On the double-action side of the coin, there are few finer craftsmen than Hamilton Bowen. Among several of the custom handguns he offers, the Alpine model is one of the most superbly created revolvers I've seen. In his Louisville, Tennessee, shop, Hamilton begins with a Ruger Redhawk, converting it to .45 Long Colt. The gripframe is reshaped, and other general polishing, beveling and filing is done. A four-inch custom bar-barrel is fitted, and the action is fine-tuned. Although Hamilton does fine grip work, the Alpine is available with stocks by master grip maker Roy Fishpaw, which give the gun a subtle elegance. Hamilton is able to provide a combination of custom services for revolvers that are all first rate and can perform custom work to suit just about every shooter's needs.

There are a number of great pistol-smiths who perform great work on auto pistols, but Louisiana-based Jim Clark is still at the top of the list. One of my favorite handguns is an old Colt Government Model .45 that I inherited from my dad. This gun was completely worked over by Jim Clark. It is the slickest, most finely tuned automatic I've ever seen and has never malfunctioned after firing thousands of rounds of ammunition. After Jim completed his custom work, the pistol was later engraved by Jim Riggs making it an extremely appealing piece of work.

These are just a few examples of what an outstanding "one gun" might be for me, but I know that some shooters just aren't concerned with customizing. Fortunately for them, the vast majority of good, new-in-the-box handguns these days are perfectly acceptable as they are. One of my fellow border lawmen, Donnie Bynum, is perfectly happy with his Glock .40-caliber pistol as an everyday gun, both for law-enforcement work as well as guiding on Texas whitetail, turkey and exotic hunts. He finds the pistol accurate, easy to handle and great for brush work. Donnie recently took an aoudad at 110 yards with a head shot from his Glock, achieving a clean, one-shot kill. Again, personal taste is the rule. He likes the pistol, shoots it well and carries it exclusively.

As for me, I'm still relishing in the fact that my work allows me to carry and shoot an uncommon variety of firearms—a truly appealing opportunity. If the time ever does come for me to have to choose just one, I'll assure you it'll be a dandy.

G&A August 1998

CHAPTER 18

The Backyard Range

Little did I know it at the time, but my upbringing in the border country of Texas and New Mexico was a true privilege, one that would, unfortunately, be difficult to duplicate today. When I was about 10 we moved from west Texas to a place near Deming, New Mexico, near the Florida Mountains. Our home was out in the country and neighbors were scarce. The location provided a perfect opportunity for a boy with interests in guns, hunting and horses.

Shortly after moving into the new place, several projects were initiated under the supervision of my Dad. The first thing was putting in a good set of corrals, a shed and a small hay barn for the horses. Next was the construction of an effective shooting range behind the house. Dad had wanted a 30-yard range right off the back porch, give or take a few feet. We paced off the distance and went to work, building the backstop out of heavily creosoted cross ties Dad had procured from a friend who worked for the railroad.

In a short time I became very well acquainted with a set of posthole diggers, excavating two large holes in which we placed two sets of cross ties as posts. We then dropped cross-ties in between the two sets of posts, resulting in a solid wall about six feet high. With hands blistered from the posthole digging, I then shoveled dirt behind our backstop, piling it all the way to the top to stop any bullets that might negotiate their way in between the ties. The result was an excellent backstop that doubled as a target stand. Multiple paper targets could be stapled right to the cross-ties.

Dad used the backyard range to test hundreds of handguns and fire thousands of rounds of ammunition throughout the years-and I learned to shoot there. Dad had instilled firearms safety in me virtually from the time I was born and had me shooting handguns at a very early age. Being able to shoot in the backyard anytime I wanted literally propelled me into the pleasure of shooting.

Our first Christmas after moving to New Mexico was splendid as I received my first handgun-a Colt .22 Single Action with a hand carved holster from Garrett Allen Saddlery. I wouldn't venture a guess as to how many rounds I fired with the little Colt, but I thought at the time that I must be keeping Winchester in business. I practiced every day in the back yard for months.

Once Dad decided I was pretty competent with the Colt, he permitted me to venture into the desert behind the house with it-after I had completed the New Mexico hunter safety course. Fricasseed cottontail was one of the family favorites, and it was rare that I didn't return from one of my excursions with a rabbit or two that had fallen to my Colt.

When I got the itch for a little variety in my shooting, Dad would usually accommodate my interests as he kept quite a selection of guns around. My favorites were always single-action revolvers. Dad had a Ruger Black Hawk in .45 Long Colt that was accompanied by a cylinder in .45 ACP. The old man had acquired two large crates containing several thousand rounds of loose military surplus .45 ACP.

Each afternoon I routinely took a 5-pound coffee can and scooped .45ACP ammo out of the crates, firing it gleefully in the backyard. A coffee can full would generally keep me shooting for 30 or 40 minutes and my skills improved significantly.

As time passed, the .45 ACP surplus was depleted and I moved on to other interests, specifically black powder guns. A Thompson Center .50 caliber Hawken flintlock and a Navy Arms .36 caliber flintlock pistol replaced the Ruger, at least for a while, and the black powder smoke made the backyard look like a Civil War battleground. I would come in the house each evening after a session of shooting, face and hands black from the residue.

After years of daily shooting in the back yard, the unthinkable happened. Neighbors moved in. A house was built about a mile south of our place, in the general direction of our daily firing. We reinforced the backstop, replacing several of the bullet-worn cross-ties. Our shooting continued, but with much concern for the new neighbors. Unfortunately, that wasn't the end of it. Before we knew it, another home was being built, then another. I resorted to shooting more trap and spending more time out in the desert.

When the time finally came for me to leave home and head off to college, Dad was still using the backyard range, but he worried constantly that it would soon have to come to an end.

A few years later, I was accepted to the New Mexico State Police Academy and Dad decided that I needed to brush up on my revolver skills in preparation for the academy. He invited me over each evening to practice with a Smith & Wesson K-22. My skills sharpened quickly and the extra practice later paid off. It was the last time I used the backyard Range.

Now that country is covered with homes and paved roads. It's growing faster everyday, and shooting doesn't seem to be an activity that young boys take part in everyday anymore, though it should be. My mother still lives at the old home place, and the old backstop is still there. It is now adorned with cow skulls and Southwestern memorabilia and was sagging a bit the last time I saw it.

To me, it's a shrine.

G&A January 2001

Section III

CHAPTER 19

Hot Competitions

To pronounce that relations among many of the residents along the U.S./Mexico line are sometimes a little turbulent would be akin to stating that A.J. Foyt likes to tinker with cars. Many people who live away from the border area are oblivious to the fact that a certain amount of consternation is the order for everyday life along our southern boundary, especially for area law enforcement personnel. And when it comes to comparing the perspectives of U.S. cops vs. their counterparts in Mexico, things get even more arduous.

There are times when differences can be disregarded and similarities nourished. One of the most celebrated of these times for border law enforcement folks is the quarterly firearms qualification. Many of the agencies and stations along the border consider qualification essentially a holiday, with shooting taking place throughout the day and a *pachanga* (barbeque) held immediately afterward. This practice is quite common on both sides of the Rio Grand in Texas, Chihuahua, Coahuila and Tamaulipas. Not infrequently, officers from various departments on both sides attend these gatherings for both the shooting events and the cookouts whereupon *esprit de corps* is developed and practiced.

My old friend, fellow shooter and retired lawman, Wilder R. Dresser, was at the beginning of his career in the early 1960's as a Border Patrol agent stationed in Del Rio, Texas. Being an avid handgun enthusiast and bulls eye shooter, Wilder was in hog heaven during qualification time as it presented unparalleled opportunities to shoot and consort with shooters. It was during one of these shoots that Wilder became acquainted with several of the avid *pistoleros* from the Cd. Acuna, Coahuila, police department and was later invited to attend a formal pistol shoot and *pachanga* at the Cd. Acuna rod and gun club. This prestigious gathering consisted of several different stages of pistol shooting intermingled with barbeque and, upon completion of the competition, libations. Contestants consisted of lawmen and other dignitaries from both sides of the river.

Mexican officials have always had a great affinity for the Colt Government Model auto pistol, especially in .38 Super. In Mexico, the military for years was issued the .45 Government Model therefore making that caliber unauthorized for law enforcement use. It is not uncommon to see officials in Mexico carrying .38 Super Colts bearing

Bart Skelton

elaborate grips, engraving and other fancy setups. The Government Model has been popular enough in Mexico that pistol courses designed specifically for that particular gun have been developed, among these the infamous Yaqui Defense Course.

The Yaqui Defense Course, one of the favorite courses of the Mexican police and the one concentrated on during Wilder's visit to Cd. Acuña, requires that the shooter be extremely adept with the single action auto pistol. The concept of the course is simple, but very difficult to execute and master. The shooter takes a stance about three feet from the target, a standard paper silhouette, and addresses it with the pistol in the strong hand, slide locked back with an empty magazine in the well. The pistol is then pointed at the target and canted at an angle allowing the ejection port to face skyward. The shooter then takes six rounds of loose .45 Auto or .38 Super in his left hand and prepares for the engagement. The course requires that the shooter fire the shots in a nine second time period by dropping a round into the open chamber, releasing the slide and firing into the target, repeating this procedure six times over.

The Yaqui course can be somewhat hazardous to the shooter, as it is almost impossible to actually keep an eye on the target while manipulating the pistol. The shooter must maintain eye contact (unless he is extremely dexterous) with the pistol while dropping in the rounds and pressing the correct levers. Since the ejection port faces upward, the empties are often cast directly into the shooter's face, making the task even more demanding.

Wilder's visit to the Acuña rod and gun club was enhanced by the presence of the sub-comandante of the municipal police department, a pleasant man of considerable size who relished in participating in all area pistol shoots. The sub-comandante showed up in his most handsome Class-A police regalia for the shoots and prided himself as one of the best Yaqui Defense shooters in the country.

When all betting, toasts and other prescribed luck wishing was adjourned, the match finally commenced. As can be envisioned, the shooting was difficult and many of the competitors were unable to fire their six shots in the imposed time frame. When at last the sub-comandante stepped up to the line, he confidently drew his Colt and carefully positioned the six rounds in his left hand in a fashion that they could be loaded with lightning speed. When the whistle blew, the big lawman wasted no time and the shots began ringing. But after the third shot, it was apparent that something was amiss. The sub-comandante began jumping up and down, grumbling and blowing mightily through his nose, all the while not missing a lick of shooting. After the sixth shot was expelled, the sub-comandante immediately turned away from his target and thrust his empty slabside into his waistband. His face was twisted in pain and a small trail of smoke curled from his nose- it was immediately obvious to the rest of the shooters what had occurred.

When the sub-comandante had successfully removed the scalding piece of brass from his left nostril, the crowd was taken back. He had done a remarkable job of firing the six shots within time limit, held an outstanding six shot group meanwhile enduring the agony of the fiery empty case lodged against his septum.

After the match, guns were put away, barbeque eaten and homage paid to the bravery of the sub-comandante, whose love for the shooting game is still talked about on the border.

G&A July 1998

CHAPTER 20

Different Worlds

When many people think about existence in the Southwest acreage, the topic that often comes to mind is the fierce lifestyle that existed in the expanse for so long. Historical anecdote spinning has turned the Southwest—and the Western states in general- into a rather abstruse place that brings wild lawlessness and violence to those whose preoccupation lends itself to such matter. For the most part those notions are just memories these days, at least on the north side of the U.S.-Mexican border. But the situation on the south side is a bit more profound.

Through my escapades as a lawman near the border over the last several years, I have had the fortune to become acquainted with a number of police officers of various designation in the Mexican states of Chihuahua and Coahuila. As a result of these acquaintances, I have learned that Mexico-and especially Mexican border towns-aren't lacking in violence that equals or exceeds that of the lawless American West of the 1800's.

One of the attributes of Mexican police officers, at least most of the ones I have known, is that they have a great interest in firearms. Mexican laws are extremely severe when it comes to firearms ownership, meaning basically that the common citizen is banned from owning one. Exceptions are made for those in agricultural services such as farmers and ranchers who can justify owning a .22 rifle for predator control. Other exceptions are in effect for gun clubs; the government allows certain exemption for guns used in silhouette shooting, which is quiet fashionable in Mexico. But middle class citizens are pretty much out of luck when it comes to firearms-ownership. This might be one of the reasons that many Mexican police officers are quite taken with guns-they are about the only ones, besides the military, who can have one.

Most Mexican officers and agents fancy the auto pistol, many thinking highly of the .45 auto, which is strictly reserved for military use. For years, Mexican lawmen have been big fans of the .38 Super in lieu of the .45, and more recently the 10mm has become very popular, especially among elements of the Federal Judicial Police. A few years ago, one of my acquaintances on the other side of the border, Ricardo, summoned me down for a visit, which I cordially accepted. The agent had just acquired a new Colt Delta Gold Cup 10mm auto pistol, which he was carrying on duty .

I accompanied Ricardo to a remote spot outside of town fired a few boxes of Hydra-Shoks through the beautiful new pistol. A few weeks later Ricardo telephoned me again and invited me across the border for dinner and refreshments, but my schedule would not permit the trip. The next day, I learned that misadventure had struck my friend and several of his colleagues. The group, which consisted of several Mexican Federal agents and several Chihuahua State Police agents, had been taking in refreshments at a local establishment when trouble broke out between my friend and a known narcotics trafficker. A scuffle ensued during which the Delta Gold Cup, which had been concealed under Ricardo's shirt, toppled onto the floor of the crowded cantina and quickly found its way into the hands of the trafficker. Without hesitation, the trafficker fired upon Ricardo with a barrage or shots, three which struck my friend. The trafficker then turned the 10mm upon the other agents, who were busy drawing their handguns. Ten millimeter bullets found their way into two of the other agents before they were able to fatally shoot down the trafficker. One of the agents was killed. Ricardo was taken to a local hospital with a shot to his left arm and two to others in his left side. He later told me that, although the trafficker's shots had not been in vital areas, the extreme

Bart Skelton

shock and damage inflicted by the 10mm Hydra-Shoks had caused him to almost bleed to death.

One of the most disturbing aspects of this story is that it occurred in a crowded establishment that is frequented by American citizens who would never dream that such a situation might take place. I don't know how many shots were actually fired, but it was a mystery that none of the onlookers were killed or injured. This type of scenario occurs more often than many people realize. Even though the casualties in this incident were inflicted by Ricardo's own pistol, it doesn't mean that that is always the case. Mexican criminal organizations are rampant on the U. S.-Mexican line, and firearms are readily available, even though they are illegal. Gangland-style shootings take place with disturbing frequency in places like Cd. Juarez, Chihuahua. American citizens insisting on visiting such places must use caution and be aware of their surrounding at all times.

Along with being wary, Americans planning to visit Mexico must ensure that they are not carrying any type of firearms or ammunition. Recently, there has been a considerable amount of media attention on incidents along the border that involve Americans being arrested at the border on Mexican side in possession of firearms and/or ammunition. One man was recently convicted in Cd. Juarez for possession of a deer rifle and ammunition and sentenced to five years in prison.

He is one of many. The worst part of this individual's situation is that he had crossed into Mexico unintentionally; within a few moments, he went from a place where carrying a firearm is perfectly acceptable and legal to a place where an unimaginably terrible jail cell was his reward for the same act.

Though many aspects of travel to Mexico may seem appealing, be cautious if you must go. There are some things down in the border country that haven't changed.

G&A January 1999

CHAPTER 21

Comandante's Pachanga

For many years a romantic magnetism has drawn *Americanos* southward into the expansive deserts of Mexico. Something about the way of living down there seems tranquil to many and life seems to be enjoyed at a much slower pace. But that same tranquility can quickly turn deadly, a fact that many visitors to that country don't seem to be aware of. It's true that when one ventures south of the border into Mexico, it's like stepping back in time. Day-to-day life is much different, much slower, and human life is of little significance.

I find myself among those who bear that strange enchantment with Mexico and its way of life, though I now visit there infrequently due to my growing unpopularity among various factions of drug traffickers. But a few years ago, I traveled into northern Chihuahua quite regularly and developed a good liaison with elements of the Chihuahua State Police Department. My initial encounters with the Chihuahua agents were formal and at times rather tense. I was leery of them, mostly because of the stories I had always heard about certain unsavory investigative techniques used by the Mexican police. As I came to know many of them more personally I found them to be a light-hearted bunch, always eager to celebrate my arrival with a cookout and/or a pistol shoot.

Bart Skelton

One Saturday morning in October a few years back, I received a call from the Comandante in Las Palomas, Chihuahua, inviting me down for a *pachanga* (cookout). I accepted the offer and later made the 30-mile trip down to the little border town. Upon arriving at the *comandancia* (state police headquarters), located on a dusty street on the outskirts of the town, I found my counterparts unloading a pickup truck laden with mesquite, which was later piled into a large hole in the ground and set afire. About an hour and a half later, the mesquite had burned down to a beautiful set of pungent coals over which a steel grate was placed. After allowing the grate to become white-hot, large beefsteaks, were thrown on the fire and seasoned, officially marking the start of our *pachanga*. Iced-down Carta Blanca beer was ushered in on a dolly pushed by a young man from a nearby cantina. As the steaks sizzled over the hot mesquite, stories and jokes began flowing.

Before the actual feast began, we were joined by several members of the municipal police, three young birds who were new to police work and had never had any formal police training. The *municipales* were excited almost to the point of being frantic and were soliciting help from the Comandante. It seemed that a local hoodlum had gone crazy and holed himself up in a nearby shack where he was threatening to kill his wife with a machete. The *municipales* related to the Comandante that upon their arrival at the scene, the rowdy man had threatened them with the machete. The Comandante inquired of the three why they had not just shot the man and been done with the matter. The three simply stared at the Comandante with blank looks on their faces. The Comandante then advised them that he and his crew were busy and that they would have to resolve the matter on their own.

The mesquite seared steaks were delectable. They were served with fresh corn tortillas and a fiery *pico de gallo* salsa, washed down with ice-cold Carta Blanca. The fall evening was cool and quiet—great barbecuing weather. More steaks were thrown on the grill, but the corn tortillas had not lasted long. The Comandante ordered one of the agents, Ernesto, to head to the town bakery and procure more. Ernesto gestured for me to accompany him and we hopped in the old pickup and headed down the severely rutted road leading downtown. Before arriving at the bakery we noticed a gathering of local citizens in front of an old adobe home on a side street, prompting Ernesto to investigate. As we pulled up the residence, we quickly spotted the three young *municipales* standing in the yard of the house. They looked relieved when they saw Ernesto. They explained that the crazy fellow was still in the house threatening to kill his wife and that they had attempted to break the door down, to no avail.

Ernesto shook his head and advised the three youngsters that he was about to give them a quick lesson in hostage negotiation. He exited the truck, slinging an M-16 rifle over his shoulder. The crowd moved out of his way as he headed toward the front door. Ernesto calmly announced that he was a state police agent and that he demanded the release of the woman. The crazy man quickly glanced out the front window and saw an impatient Ernesto standing there with the M-16, which was still slung over his shoulder. The front door quickly opened and the terrified woman was shoved out, the door immediately slamming behind her. Ernesto then demanded that the perpetrator come out and give himself up.

"You will kill me if I come out," the man yelled.

Ernesto glanced back at the *municipales* and rolled his eyes. The front door opened again and the machete was tossed out.

"I'm not going to kill you. Just come out and give yourself up." Ernesto said.

A short time later, the door opened and the man slowly shuffled out with his hands raised in the air, a scared look on his face. Ernesto approached him, smiled and patted the man on the shoulder.

"See there, I told you I wasn't going to kill you," Ernesto said, still smiling.

Bart Skelton

Ernesto then turned around, hesitated, unslung the rifle and with a spinning motion turned and butt-stroked the man across the jaw, knocking him senseless. Re-slinging the rifle over his shoulder, Ernesto quietly walked past the *municipales* without acknowledging them and got back in the truck. Without another word, we drove on to the bakery.

As we walked in the cool dusk down the dusty street into the bakery, Ernesto turned to me and said, "The tortillas had better be fresh."

They were, thank goodness.

G&A January 2000

CHAPTER 22

Seafood Soup and Cocaine

It had been another scorcher in southern New Mexico, unseasonably hot for late September when the temperatures are normally cooling off some. As the sun dropped, the temperature followed and it turned into a perfect evening as I sat waiting for an old friend at one of my favorite watering holes in Mesilla, New Mexico. The beautiful, rugged, Organ Mountains were changing color with the sunset and had at last turned a deep, bluish purple when Carl showed up.

I've had the good fortune of working with some outstanding officers and agents all over the country from a variety of different law enforcement agencies. New Mexico State Police Narcotics Agent Carl Work is no exception. Carl, like most good cops, is a product of the old days and the old time way of enforcing the law, which, in my view, was the right way. Unfortunately, today's peace officers are frequently trained by bureaucrats and are restricted from doing an effective job due to excessive red tape and sheer baloney.

It had been awhile since Carl and I had visited and as he sat down, I couldn't help but thinking he looked more like a bouncer in a biker bar than a lawman. After he had eased his large frame into a chair and ordered a cool one, Carl's conversation progressed into tales of his recent adventures in the world of a New Mexico narcotics officer.

Bart Skelton

It seemed that a gang of southern New Mexico based drug traffickers had found themselves in a big hurry to unload a freshly received batch of cocaine and turn a fast profit. Through an informant, Carl had been introduced to the group and quickly engaged in a *transa,* or deal. After a lengthy, paperwork-laden official request for *buy* money, Carl and his partner finally were granted permission by the higher-ups to make the deal happen. The plan was, of course, to buy a kilo of dope from the first level dealers, then work their way up to the guys in charge, making a larger buy and later taking them all down on conspiracy charges.

Calls were made to the traffickers and plans for the transaction were set. They would meet in a seedy section of town, not far from La Mesilla, to do the deal. As usual, Carl's crew was shorthanded and a minimal number of backup/surveillance agents were available. That night, the deal was done. Carl and his partner, Larry Chavez, handed over the money and a small package was given over in exchange. The agents shook hands with the crooks and all went their separate ways.

Carl and Larry headed straight back to their office to enter their purchase into evidence. The first order of business was to weigh the dope. The agents were chagrined when the white stuff came up three ounces short of a full kilo.

Many cops would have continued on without much concern, happy that a successful transaction had taken place at all. But Carl and Larry aren't just any cops. A deal is a deal and three ounces of cocaine is worth some money.

"Absolutely nuthin' worse than a dishonest dope dealer." Carl advised me with a serious look in his eye. The coke trafficker's eyes were as big as cherry pies when his front door came crashing off its hinges. No doubt he believed his time had come. His expression turned to shock when he saw that the aggressors were Carl and Larry, and they weren't wearing any kind of police gear. Shock turned to fear when Carl, in his persuasive manner, brought the matter of the missing three ounces to the doper's attention.

86

"I demanded my money back." Carl told me. "There was a lot of stuttering and runaround, but after a little inducement, he agreed, though he said the money had already been moved."

Persistence is a virtue in law enforcement work, and Carl gave his rival a good dose of it for several days after the initial fiasco. The panicky trafficker admitted to Carl that the money had been moved to Albuquerque, about three hours to the north, and that he was making arrangements for Carl to meet the *jefe* who had actually owned the cocaine. It was later decided that Carl and Larry could meet the *jefe* in Albuquerque and set the deal straight, plus purchase another kilo- a full one this time- from them . Carl was later advised by the Albuquerque *jefe* that they didn't like to lose customers and that everything would work out.

The Siete Mares (seven seas) Restaurant in Albuquerque, New Mexico is well known for its Mexican style seafood dishes, specializing in *caldo de mariscos,* seafood soup. As Carl, Larry and the Mesilla boy waited inside the Siete Mares, a good dose of the *caldo* was making its way onto the front of the Mesilla boy's shirt as he nervously attempted to spoon it into his mouth, spoon trembling uncontrollably. He was clearly apprehensive about the meeting with the *jefe*.

"When the *jefe* came in, it was plain that something was up." Carl said. "He had his four brothers with him and was wearing a jacket - and it was summertime. Generally a good indicator."

After the *jefe* and his boys had bought a round or two for Carl and Larry and had jovially entertained them for a bit, apologizing for the inconvenience the Mesilla boy had caused, the invitation was made to go outside and complete the transaction. Carl and Larry knew the *jefe* was armed and both regretted having left their sidearm in their vehicle. Tensions ran high - no one was sure exactly what would happen next. Carl eased over to his pickup truck and retrieved the

Bart Skelton

flash money they were to use for the second cocaine deal, meanwhile grabbing his Smith and Wesson 5906 from under the seat.

With pistol tucked away under his left arm and a bag full of cash in his left hand, Carl approached the *jefe*, who stood with the package containing the kilo, jacket still on. In seconds, the *jefe* found himself on the ground with the Smith and Wesson intimately placed in his ear. Carl reached under the *jefe's* sweaty jacket and retrieved his gun, a Taurus eight shot .22 revolver. After help from Larry and the surveillance team, the entire crew was arrested and later thrown in jail. Conspiracy charges were filed and the case was tried. The *jefe* and crew are currently doing time in a New Mexico prison.

After I made light of the fact that the alleged, big time cocaine trafficker was just packing a .22 revolver, instead of a more powerful choice, Carl set me straight again.

".22 Long Rifle kills more people in the U.S. than any other caliber. You know that." He said.

I do know that once Carl and men like him are gone, the *jefe* and crew will be happy fellows.

February 2001

CHAPTER 23

Collecting in Mexico

Conversationalists who find themselves in circles involved in the topic of antique firearms, particularly those that played a part in the founding of the West, are often taken with the subject of Colt revolvers and Winchester rifles—and rightly so. After all, most everyone, gun enthusiast or not, knows that the old Colt "hogleg" and the lever gun are often referred to as the "guns that won the West." Although they are magnificent firearms, their roles in civilizing the western states were certainly not unassisted by a relatively wide selection of other fine small arms.

The non-Colt and Winchester antiques that 20 years ago were less impressive are now considered very collectible as research of historical data reflects that they were widely used by notable characters of the West.

Smith & Wesson, Remington, Merwin & Co., Webley, Hopkins & Allen and Forehand & Wadsworth are just a few of the manufacturers who produced what were considered excellent sidearm in those days. Smith & Wesson, who initially offered a line of nice pocket revolvers, later became Colt's leading competitor with the introduction of its .44 caliber No. 3 revolver.

By 1870, Smith & Wesson had been producing pocket guns in a variety of popular small calibers, but it was large-caliber handguns that were yearned for in the West. Smith & Wesson was aware of the need for a big bore, metallic cartridge pistol on the Frontier and in that year introduced its 3rd Model single action .44, later dubbed the American. This new revolver offered a strong, hinged frame and automatic extractor that ejected the cases from the cylinder when the gun was broken down for reloading. The American was far more advanced than anything offered by Colt or Remington at the time, although Colt in 1871 began offering its metallic cartridge conversion guns. Several variations of the Smith & Wesson American revolver later appeared, including the .44 New Model Russian and 2nd Model Russian. In 1876 the company began offering its famous .45 caliber Schofield on a commercial basis after several years of extensive military testing.

The list of famous frontier characters who at one time used the Smith & Wesson big bore single actions is surprising. The sweeping popularity of the 3rd Model in the West led it into the hands of characters like John Wesley Hardin, who used one to gun down Comanche, Texas County Deputy Charley Webb in 1874. Jesse James was packing a Smith & Wesson .45 1st Model Schofield at the time of his murder by Bob Ford in 1882. Famous El Paso, Texas City Marshal Dallas Stoudenmire also favored the Smith big-bore single action and was carrying a .44 American at the time of his shooting death in El Paso. It was allegedly an engraved Smith.

Another surprising fact from that era was the fierce competition that Smith & Wesson encountered in the West concerning its fine line of small caliber revolvers. The "British Bulldog", manufactured by P. Webley & Son, was a powerful little double-action revolver that was available in .-32 S&W .38 S&W and .44 Webley. The little revolver was immensely popular and widely copied by firms such as Forehand & Wadsworth, who offered their version of the "Improved British Bulldog," which they claimed could spit "seven shots in five seconds". The Bulldog type revolver was used by many renowned characters including members of the Dalton gang, and John H.

Tunstall, the Lincoln County rancher who was mysteriously murdered near Las Cruces, New Mexico just prior to the onset of the Lincoln County wars.

As most antique gun devotees are aware, a large number of firearms of every type were shipped to Mexico in the 1800s, and occasionally they can still be found floating around, though extraction of the guns from that country can be touchy, to say the least. A few years back, I had the good fortune to be introduced to a gentleman from Chihuahua City, Chihuahua, Mexico who was an attorney for the state run police department. He was conducting state business in the border town of Las Palomas, Chihuahua, directly across the line from the port of Columbus, New Mexico. An acquaintance of mine from the Chihuahua State Police had asked me the favor of escorting the attorney into the village of Columbus for a tour through the Pancho Villa Museum, to which I gladly agreed.

During the tour of the museum, my attorney friend became excited over a replica of a Smith & Wesson " American .44 revolver that was hanging on the museum wall. He explained to me that he was interested in old guns and that he had an extensive collection at his home in Chihuahua that included an original, nickel plated Smith & Wesson American bearing *cachas de marfil* (ivory grips). I explained to the gentleman that I, too, had an interest in old guns, though my collection wasn't too impressive.

The end of the afternoon found us sipping margaritas in a small cantina in dusty Palomas. The attorney advised that he was grateful for the tour of Columbus and that he would be glad to part with his old Smith & Wesson for the sake of friendship.

As I walked through the rough little town of Palomas on my way back to the port of entry that evening, I contemplated a trip down to Chihuahua City to see my new acquaintance to possibly acquire the old .44. I further considered the complications of such a trip and the likelihood of bad trouble. I finally envisioned myself sitting in a Mexican juzgado trying to explain why I had a Smith & Wesson .44

Bart Skelton

hidden under the seat of my truck, which was now being driven by various elements of the local police department after being seized for transporting contraband. I concluded that the old American might be better off remaining in Mexico.
Life on the border isn't always fair.

G&A June 1999

CHAPTER 24

Hector's .45

Border characters seem to always carry with them a certain amount of charisma no matter which side of the law their sentiments may seem to be. I've run into characters of every type during my escapades along the border, and I'll tell you that even some of the outlaws have been rather intriguing. Many of these encounters have been in the company of my fellow lawman and running mate Miguel Briseño.

Miguel has worked the brush country on both sides of the U.S./Mexico line for more than 22 years and is the quintessential desert rat. His ability to work the border residents for various types of information is legendary. This expertise, which I suppose is referred to these days as "networking," has netted Miguel intelligence leading to large scale investigations that resulted in significant arrests, as well as information leading to the whereabouts of great bargains on various categories of antique firearms.

A great deal of Briseño's networking has taken place in the dismal little town of General Rodrigo M. Quevedo—or as it is commonly known, Puerto Palomas, Chihuahua—located across the line from Columbus, New Mexico. A dark reminder of the penurious economy of our southern neighbor, Palomas is a sanctuary for smugglers, con artists and criminals of just about every variety. A dusty town bearing about 8,000 denizens, no paved streets, 25 cantinas and all the trouble one could imagine mustering, this small border borough teems with activity 24 hours a day. It is common to hear gunfire throughout town most every night generated from a variety of sources, mostly drug related. Although illegal in Mexico, firearms of every conceivable type are fashionable and common in Palomas.

Frequenting some of Palomas' finer drinking establishments has proven to be an excellent way to gather information or just to get a look at some of northern Chihuahua's "Who's Who" of narcotic smugglers. Miguel Briseño has actually befriended several of the establishment owners, a good idea since their clientele are rarely friendly toward American lawmen.

One autumn afternoon, Miguel and I happened into one of the more famous Palomas cantinas that was owned and operated by the flamboyant Hector. Hector had no use for American cops and made no attempt to camouflage that bias, even though he had once carried a commission as a police agent in Palomas. He did enjoy occasionally gabbing with Miguel about some of the local hearsay and wrongdoing. The more ice-cold Mexican beer Hector drank, the more graphic the chat would become. Upon our arrival this particular day, Hector had laid back a good portion of a bottle of brandy and was in good humor, actually welcoming us into the place with icy beer on the house.

After a few yarns about the local happenings, the conversation turned to guns. Hector, like many Palomas residents, was a fancier of handguns and owned several. Miguel had learned through his sources that the colorful barman owned an old Colt Government Model .45 with ivory stocks carved with the Mexican snake and eagle, and Miguel was convinced that he could beat the barman out of the old slabside. But Hector insisted that the Colt was no longer in his possession, a result of an unfortunate incident that had taken place across the street from his bar, which happened to be the Palomas municipal police department and jailhouse.

It seems that two of Hector's female employees had become associated with two malefactors from Janos, a small town near the city of Casas Grandes. The two had been in Palomas recruiting locals to run loads of marijuana into the United States. Hector agreed to transport a load and make some extra cash on the side, but had been hornswoggled, losing the illegal grass to another competing smuggler before reaching the U.S. side. This infuriated the Janos boys, who took revenge on the two women by beating them half to death. Upon learning of the episode, the outraged Hector contacted the local police *comandante* and demanded that the two offenders be arrested and jailed. Indeed, the *comandante* took action, locating the two and incarcerating them in the decrepit Palomas jail located just a few yards from Hector's establishment.

That evening, Hector sat drinking in his cantina, gazing across the street at the rundown building that imprisoned his antagonists. He agonized over the situation until he could stand it no more. He dashed home and retrieved the ivory-handled Colt and extra magazines. He designated his wife to drive what Hector affectionately called the "getaway car," a 1975 Pontiac station wagon, himself swilling brandy and cuddling the .45. They drove up to the jail and Hector exited the getaway car, dashing inside with .45 at ready. He confronted the only officer on duty and ran him out of the building at gunpoint. He then proceeded to the cell that contained one of the offenders, stuck the pistol through the door and fired erratically, several rounds striking the terrified smuggler. Hector then ran through the smoke-filled office and to the car, making a swift departure. As they drove away, Hector realized that the other smuggler had been left unharmed in the cell next to the one he had just assaulted. Figuring that he was in trouble anyway, Hector ordered his wife to drive them back to the jail for a second attack. He again entered the office, jammed the pistol through the second door and fired another full magazine, but missed the smuggler entirely. He then jumped in the car and departed.

Although thoroughly questioned about the incident, Hector was never charged with the assault on the jail.

Miguel and I quietly listened to the story, questioning the veracity of every word until Hector produced a clipping from the Casas Grandes

Bart Skelton

newspaper outlining the event much the way the barman himself had. In Miguel's eyes, the shooting escapade had increased the value of the Colt and certainly his desire to own it. Hector passed on not long ago, and I suspect that his ivory handled shooter is still down on the border somewhere.

G&A April 1998

CHAPTER 25

Bisley blowups.

For all of its strife, turbulence and generally bad times, I have maintained a fascination with the desert country of northern Chihuahua, Mexico. The desert mountains and lush scenery combined with a relatively primitive way of life are alluring to me.

It was a blazing-hot July afternoon years ago when my old border rat partner Miguel Briseño and I were conducting some police liaison business in the dusty little town of Las Palomas, Chihuahua situated right on the borderline south of Columbus, New Mexico. We paid the new state judicial police comandante a visit regarding a pair of drug-smuggling suspects of ours who had been ducking us for some time.

Miguel and I had maintained an excellent association with the Chihuahua State Police agents and their previous comandante, and our arrival at their offices had almost always called for a festive pachanga or pistol shoot of some sort, which preceded any business talk.

But this new comandante was different. Upon announcing our arrival, we were asked to wait outside of the building for some time before being escorted into the comandante's office, a small, dingy affair painted in dull gray. The comandante, a large, repugnant man dressed in a sweat soaked T-shirt, sat at his desk eyeballing us with displeasure. The wall behind him was lined with several AK47's and

97

M16 rifles, issue guns for his agents. The room smelled of gun oil, sweat and stale alcohol. Miguel politely explained to the comandante the purpose of our visit, apologizing for such an inconvenience.

The comandante seemed to pay little attention to our request for assistance in our case, concerning himself more with the condition of his fingernails, which he constantly scraped with a small pen knife. After becoming bored with the pen knife, the comandante searched his desk drawer for a new plaything. Upon discovering and withdrawing from the desk his next trinket, the comandante's eyes lit up some, as did Miguel's and mine.

From the old metal desk, the comandante retrieved a blued, case hardened Colt Bisley Model .45 bearing a 7 1/2-inch barrel and one-piece pearl stocks. He carefully placed the hammer at half cock and gently turned the cylinder. After seeing that the old six-shooter was empty, the comandante aimed the old six-gun at an outdated Carta Blanca calendar, the only wall-hanging in the office and dry-fired several times.

Bisleys in that kind of condition are hard to come by and the thought of this one to slip through our fingers was not admissible. The comandante laid the revolver on the desk in front of him, exposing it to the light and our field view. The Colt was in fine condition, crisp case colors, little wear on the barrel and bright-blue screws—an excellent honest-wear Bisley.

I seized the opportunity to practice my Spanish politely querying the comandante concerning the history of the Colt. He explained in an unenthusiastic monotone that a nearby community at the base of the mountains near Janos, Chihuahua had been recently terrorized by a woman who packed the old gun in her belt. It had been necessary for his men to disarm her and jail her for certain horrors that she had committed. The comandante instructed us that the old revolver was really not good for anything as it was just to old and not powerful enough. The comandante states that the gun would be retired to the wall as a souvenir.

Our attempts to inquire as to any means that the old Colt might be appropriated, at great benefit to the comandante, of course, were originally rebuffed. But some headway was made when the comandante agreed to join us for dinner at a local establishment, during which we fed him and his assistant a large meal of steak ranchera, washed down with liberal mount of El Presidente brandy. Police stories were told, lies were swapped, and bad jokes were endured. The Colt Bisley was brought up more than once. The comandante, bearing generous portions of salsa *ranchera* on the front of his shirt, seemed to be more at ease with us. He finally agreed to remit to us the old Bisley for a nominal figure, which included a new blender for his wife who resided south of Chihuahua City, if we agreed to return the following Saturday. We were elated.

After our trip to Wal-Mart on Saturday morning for the purchase of a fine new Hamilton-Beach blender, Miguel and I drove the 35 miles to Las Palomas, gleefully contemplating our trade. We parked on the U.S. side and walked across the border making our way through the dusty Saturday morning traffic in downtown Las Palomas, our trail leading us directly in front of the Las Palomas Municipal Police Department. The local *municipales (*street cops) in Las Palomas are more or less hired off of the street with little or no experience in police work and are generally tasked with minor peacekeeping in the local brothers. Uniform attire is Levi's and whatever shirt can be found. Side arms are equally oddball.

As we passed by the police office, we decided to drop by and say hello to the officers inside, one of which had been an acquaintance of Miguel's. The men were inside, gathered around a desk inspecting a firearm. We eased closer to the group, said hello and glared wide-eyed at the object of their attention. Miguel and I looked at each other in shock, fathoming that our trade had come to a dreadful end.

"The comandante loaned us this old *pistola* for some target practice." exclaimed the captain, showing off the piece of twisted metal that was once our beautiful Colt.

"This ammunition we had for it was too strong, though. Francisco is still at the doctor's office from shooting it."

It seemed that young Francisco had wrapped the .44 Magnum ammunition with black electrician tape to make the cartridges fit into the cylinder of the .45 Bisley. After the third round, the Bisley's top strap had been destroyed, along with the pearl stocks.

Miguel and I whiled away the rest of our Saturday mixing margaritas with our new Hamilton-Beach blender, contemplating the strange way of life down on the border.

G&A April 1999

CHAPTER 26

A Lawyer's Little Colt

The dust was blowing in from the west in great clouds, stirring up trash and tumbleweeds and causing them to pile up against fences and buildings. It wasn't enough of a littering to cause a real eyesore in the bustling little town of Las Palomas, Chihuahua, because the streets there always garnished with a generous amount of refuse. The strong west wind just relocated things enough so that it was like a temporary redecoration, causing little concern to the citizenry.

Our interest in a particularly unsavory segment of the Palomas community led my old border partner, Miguel Briseño, and I to the dirty little town that spring day. Las Palomas is well known along the entire border as a hotbed of smuggling activity, as well as a gathering site for those preferring to stray from the criminal code of silence.

Miguel and I had received a tip indicating that certain individuals from the interior of the state Chihuahua had been planning a smuggling escapade through the Palomas area. Miguel and I had decided to look up a couple of our Mexican counterparts from the Chihuahua State Police and hopefully share some information concerning the bunch. Upon our arrival in Palomas, the Mexican agents had asked us to join them at the Lucky Seven, a popular Palomas establishment that doubled as a second office to our Mexican police *compañeros*.

101

As luck would have it, the state police boys had brought with them an attorney from their prosecution staff who was visiting from out of town. The state police agents introduced the gentleman to us as El Lic (short for *licenciado*, a Spanish term for attorney). El Lic was a likeable fellow, though he had obviously had an early start on the Carta Blanca.

After some conversation, it was pointed out to El Lic that Miguel and I were both fanciers of firearms. The *licenciado's* eyes brightened and he quickly broke into a discourse concerning his own interest in guns and a rundown of his extensive collection that he kept down in Chihuahua City.

The conversation turned to defensive handguns, and the *licenciado* reached down the back of his pants and withdrew a handgun. The patrons of the Lucky Seven within spitting distance turned and bolted through the front door, no doubt accustomed to such activity and not interested in being a part of it. The *licenciado* stood holding a Colt 1903 Pocket, staring at it affectionately. The bartender, David, was also staring at the little Colt, but the look in his eyes didn't express any sort of affection. He wanted no part of the inebriated attorney or his little automatic.

El Lic then handed me the gun. It was in excellent condition, bearing 90 percent of the original bluing and showing nothing but honest wear—a nice little collectible.

"I took it from a large-scale *narcotraficante* from Parral," said El Lic proudly. Miguel and I noticed that the Colt was chambered for .38 Colt Automatic. We exchanged glances, knowing that a deal might be easily struck with the *licenciado*, since it was probably quite difficult for him to obtain ammunition for the little auto in the U.S., much less in Mexico.

We were quick to buy El Lic another icy Carta Blanca, over which we discussed the possibility of a trade. I was curious as to where the *licenciado* might have obtained .38 Colt Auto ammo, since it's been discontinued for many years. So I asked him. "Senor, I have plenty of ammunition for the pistol," was his reply.

After a fair amount of persuasion, El Lic finally admitted that he would be willing to part with the little Colt, though the only trade he would consider would be for a Browning Hi-Power 9mm. He stated that the Hi-Power was the only pistol more effective than his Colt.

For the next few weeks, Miguel and I both attempted to ferret out a halfway decent Hi-Power. I was finally able to locate one through my old friend, Wilder R. Dresser, and though he wasn't extremely anxious to get rid of it, he figured it was for a worthy cause.

A short time later, I contacted my state police friends in Palomas and advised them that a trade was in the making. They told me that El Lic was already in our area conducting some personal business and that he had planned on stopping in to see Miguel and I, anxious to make a trade. Hours later, we were negotiating with the *Licendiado* concerning the deal.

He produced the little Colt and handed it over. Miguel examined it thoroughly, removed the magazine, then removed one of the cartridges. A look of discouragement immediately crossed his face as he handed the round to me.

It was a .38 Super. Miguel quickly unchambered the round from the gun's tube and examined the interior working, becoming even more disappointed. It was apparent that the little pistol had been fired on time too many with the powerful .38 Super stuff.

The .38 Super had been designed as an improvement over the .38 Colt Automatic round, and the two are very close in dimension. But, El Lic's small-frame pistol had not been designed for the extra punishment of the .38 Super, especially over a prolonged period of time. The barrel was in dangerously bad shape and the extractor was gone, undoubtedly blown off from the pressures. The firing pin had also been broken.

Miguel and I returned home, and with a little coaxing and a good bottle of sour mash, I was able to convince Wilder to buy back his Hi-Power. Unfortunately, our Mexican attorney friend went back to Chihuahua and spread the word about the two *Americanos'* inept and unfair gun trading practices.

Our Mexican gun-trading days quashed— or at least on hold— Miguel and I have considered the possibility of a new sideline.

Guided tours to Chihuahua are out, though.

G&A June 2000

Section IV

CHAPTER 27

Burro Tacos

In the early springtime, when the days become a little longer and warmer, many of the inhabitants of southern New Mexico begin to spend a little more time out of the house. Shooting, fooling with horses and cooking outdoors on a hot bed of mesquite coals are of few of the activities that start crossing my mind during this time of year. It was on one of those spring days some years back that I first ran into Rudy Mauldin. The wind was blowing, as it usually does in the spring, kicking up tufts of dirt and dust in the rickety old roping arena, where several Silver City cowboys used to convene twice a week to throw a loop at fast-moving *corriente* steers.

After missing all of my steers and being bucked off by my old brown horse, Rudy obligingly, and laughingly, rode up to help me out some. When Rudy, a jewel of a horseman, finally realized that my roping ability might be a lost cause, we retired to his old pickup for a cool one. I learned that Rudy had cowboy'd all of his life and had later turned to police work after tiring of the struggle to feed his family on cowhand and horseshoe wages. Rudy also filled me in on some of his hunting escapades and advised me that he had been hunting all of his life, growing up the son of a New Mexico Game and Fish officer in northern New Mexico.

"I'm pretty handy at huntin' bear with a pistol, you know," he said. "They're in season now and them little ol' kids of mine have been buggin' me for some bear tacos." I remained quiet, wondering about the palatability of bear-meat tacos. After some thought about the matter, Rudy invited me to accompany him into the Gila Wilderness for a spring bear hunt.

We met in the following days to finalize our arrangements. We packed camouflage, predator calls and other gear before we got down to the selection of firearms. I threw in a box of Garrett .44 Magnum super hard-cast stuff for use in my Ruger Redhawk, noticing that Rudy was looking at the big revolver questioningly "That's a big ol' pistol for this country, bud." he said. "Here's my bear gun."

He tossed a small revolver my direction. It was a Smith and Wesson Model 66 .357 with a 2-inch barrel and round butt. A nice little gun, but certainly not my choice for bear hunting, I was already beginning to have my doubts about this hunt.

The next morning found us unloading our horses at the Sheep Corrals, an old homestead located on the southern end of the Gila Wilderness. Our route would take us down a long and very steep descent into the

Sapillo River, an offshoot of the Gila. It would take us a good portion of the day to make our trek into Rudy's favorite bear-hunting country.

We double-checked our gear, mounted up and headed downhill, Rudy's snub-nosed neatly tucked into his jacket pocket. The sky and trees revolved through a variety of color shades as we dropped down the mountain towards the river The horses seemed to be content with the trip even though the terrain was rough and the trail precipitous. Rudy spun stories of his years working on large ranches near the Navajo reservation. We casually sipped coffee, not suspecting that the calmness of the new day was about to be upended.

The horses stopped so suddenly that Rudy and I were shaken with surprise, losing both our balance and coffee. The horses had stopped with front feet spread-eagled, heads down, eyes wide open, ears straight forward, trembling and snorting. They lunged in different directions off of the trail and into the thick scrub oak and pinon that covered the mountainside, half bucking and half leaping before stopping again to get a look at the god awful sight ascending the trail.

A little burro ascended the trail in front of a group of hikers, his ears perked as he watched our horses, and looked as if he had finally found a friend. Never had either one of us seen an animal packed with as much gear as this one. Five ice chests adorned the animal, two on each side and one extra-large one on top. Sleeping bags, suitcases, portable stereos and other gear was packed on top of the chests, dwarfing the little equine. As the burro trotted up the trail with his booty, a group of sandal-wearing environmental types chased behind, fearing that the load might topple. Upon spying our horses, the burro had obviously figured he had found an opportunity to escape the group and join some of his own.

But our horses had a different opinion of the situation. They quivered in terror. As the burro trotted towards us with its load bouncing erratically, the horses decided to take evasive action and nothing was stopping them. They ran through the brush, bucking and jumping. I lost a stirrup and my horse dragged me off underneath a pinon tree.

Rudy had become tickled at the entire situation and was laughing so hard he fell off. Our gear was scattered over the entire mountainside.

"Bud, we must have stacked a cord of fire wood comin' down that hill." Rudy laughed, looking back at the path of broken branches left by the horrified horses, from which hung tattered remnants of our gear. In the distance we then heard the faint voice of one of the environmentalists. "Heeere, Marty," the voice called. One of the sandal-sporting dudes was chasing the burro with a long switch. But Marty, with his colossal burden would have no part of his caller.

Rudy was still laughing hysterically. We were both skinned up. It took the rest of the trip to find the horses and gather up what was left of our gear. We later sat next to a pinon fire, contemplating the state of our hunt. Rudy quietly turned the cylinder of his little Model 66, which I later discovered was indeed a good bear gun—at least for him.

"How do you figure your kids would feel about burro tacos?" I asked. Rudy gave me a hard look and sat contemplating.

"Not *near* greasy enough," he replied.

G&A May 1999

CHAPTER 28

Burro suitcases?

As the Rio Grande River winds its way from New Mexico to the point of its demise near Brownsville, Texas, it passes through wild, tough country that holds a million tales. Rushing down from Southern Colorado through the center of New Mexico, the Rio Grande turns southeast at El Paso, Texas, leaving a lonely barbed wire fence to amble due west for hundreds of miles, marking the periphery of the United States and Mexico. The border country that is split by this rickety old boundary at the southern end of New Mexico, Arizona and California also has many stories to tell. The river continues to snake its way through the beautiful canyons of Big Bend National Park and later through brush country rich in history. Many of the more famous tales of wild border life seem to have taken place on the Texas/Mexico border and involve the Great River, the Rio Grande. Raids by Mexican bandits into Texas, Comanche attacks on both sides of the river and Texas Rangers' attempts to quell them are well-known stories to most students of border history. Generic banditry has continued in the Rio Grande country from the early days when the Texas Rangers were first assembled.

My own part in chasing the border crooks seems minuscule when one considers the years of effort by so many fine lawmen. One of the great rewards I have earned during my tenure as a border lawman has been my association with some fine outstanding officers and agents who have devoted their lives to fighting crime on the border. One of my most recent friendships has been with Manuel Duarte, a Texas peace officer with deep roots in West Texas ranching and law enforcement work. Recently, Manny and I were partaking in some quiet conversation after finishing a lengthy surveillance of a gang of smugglers. Manny sparked the chat with a few yarns from old timers he had known down in the river country south of Sierra Blanca, Texas, a desolate expanse of rugged mountains in West Texas. Manny went on to spin the tale of a peace officer who had ventured from his west Texas ranch to California, where he had joined a private investigator's firm. The Texan later found himself assigned to a case involving the husband of an old *tamalera,* a lady who had done well for herself in the commercial tamale business in Southern California. It seemed that her husband had bolted to Mexico with a young gal from Cuidad Juarez, Chihuahua, and the *tamalera* wanted him back home, pronto. Our young investigator quickly found himself traveling back to west Texas and was soon on the dusty streets of El Paso, preparing to cross the river and begin his pursuit of the estranged husband.

The year was 1918. Upon arriving in El Paso, the young man had first checked into the famous Paso del Norte Hotel and later stopped by the El Paso County Offices to look up the sheriff, an old acquaintance of his. The young investigator explained the reason behind his visit, asking the sheriff for advice concerning his journey into Mexico. The sheriff explained to the detective that the Mexican Revolution was still raging and that Cd. Juarez was no place for a young American dressed in a suit and tie. He went on to explain that the banditry in Juarez was such that they would likely kill him for his clothes.

The sheriff coaxed the young man into delaying, if not canceling, his trip to Juarez. He told the investigator that he and a couple of deputies were planning a little operation on the river that night and could use his help. The Sheriff explained that they had been having trouble with a particular smuggler from Juarez who had been importing heroin into El Paso. An informant had advised them that the smuggler had an ingenious approach to smuggling baseball-sized wads of the drug. The snitch's tip indicated that the smuggler was hiding the heroin in the ears of a burro. The burro would be led down to the river in the dark to a crossing familiar to the animal and turned loose. Having crossed the river at that location frequently, the burro knew that the smuggler had a spot on the U.S. side where hay and grain was put out, therefore marking the delivery point for the contraband.

That evening found the sheriff, deputies and investigator hunkered down in the brush near the burro's feed trough, waiting for delivery of the heroin. After some wait, the burro arrived as expected and dove into his reward. A short time later, a man slowly approached the area, walked up to the burro and caught him gently, removing the illegal booty from the animal's long, slender ears. As the smuggler busied himself with the heroin, the sheriff and crew quietly surrounded him and got the drop on him. The smuggler, realizing he had no chance, gave up quickly. The sheriff approached the man and disarmed him. He had been carrying a beautiful Smith and Wesson .32-20 six-inch nickel revolver bearing pearl stocks.

Later that evening, after the smuggler had been placed in the *juzgado*, the sheriff and the investigator sat discussing the escapade, admiring the fancy Smith and Wesson. The sheriff handed the revolver to the younger man, telling him to keep the gun as a souvenir of his first anti-smuggling operation.

Manny told me that the investigator had cherished the fancy Smith and Wesson for a long time after that, carrying it as his primary sidearm through a career as a U.S. Marshal for over 40 years. I looked at Manny and shook my head, telling him that the old Smith would be a great gun to have in one's collection. Manny looked at me and grinned. He tipped his hat back and said "Sure enough, and it's sitting in my safe deposit box back in Austin right now." I looked at Manny in disbelief.

"That fellow was my dad," he said.

G&A September 1999

CHAPTER 29

Grazing in the Grass

The borderlands of the extreme southern portions of New Mexico and Arizona are comprised of country that seems altogether useless to many, but is a sanctuary for others. To some, me included, this desolate area is beautiful precisely because of its isolation. And, contrary to what many folks mistakenly believe, the area teems with life.

Having experienced the border virtually from one end to the other, I am still impressed with the splendor of the New Mexico boot heel area. This region, located in the extreme southwest corner of the state, was so-named due to its resemblance to the heel of a cowboy boot when observed on a map. My familiarity with the boot heel area began about 10 years ago with my escapades involving border drug prohibition.

The expanse of the New Mexico boot heel is sparsely populated, and from just about any point inside it, at least three-fourths of a tank of gasoline is required to drive to the nearest filling station. Huge, rough mountains surround brush-filled valleys throughout the area. Drugs flow freely through it from the Mexican states of Chihuahua and Sonora. As a young investigator, I was to learn a good deal from my first encounter with the boot heel.

As has been a common occurrence in the past and will continue to be, the office rookie—me, in this case—was recruited for the task of laying on a mountaintop in the boot heel area to observe nighttime traffic in the southeast corner of the area. The detail was to last a week to 10 days and I was to be accompanied by two National Guardsmen. We were picked up by a New Mexico Air National Guard Huey helicopter for the insertion.

The NG boys were to take nothing in but a sleeping bag, water and military rations. I had decided well in advance that such provisions would not quite be sufficient and had procured an extra-large Coleman ice chest for the caper. I had filled the chest with some venison, portions of a fresh-butchered hog from the Mike Laney ranch, a good supply of fresh New Mexico green chile, tortillas and other refreshments. Along with my duty firearms, I decided it prudent to pack in my dad's old Smith and Wesson K-22 revolver and a good supply of ammo for it. I also packed a good sleeping bag with an air mattress and a pillow, as well as a good Dutch oven.

The tongue lashing from the helicopter crew chief did little to change my mind about what I felt was necessary gear, and after a good deal of haggling, he finally reluctantly tied down the ice chest with bungle cords and we took off.

Our flight into the drop-off zone was exhilarating as we observed some of the most panoramic views on the border. We circled a few mountaintops and finally, found just the right one, situated at about 7,700 feet and overlooking a huge expanse of Chihuahuan desert. The crew chief shook his head in disgust as I unloaded my pack outfit. The two NG boys and I were soon left to set up camp and admire the plains below.

The first two days were quite uneventful, and I spent most of the daylight hours on the high, rocky outcrops, occasionally plinking with the K-22. There was a small farm below about four miles away on the Chihuahua side of the border. The farm featured a very small shack

115

and was deserted during daylight. Nighttime, however, offered a completely different perspective.

At around midnight, vehicle lights could be seen coming into the small farm from every direction. The NG boys and I spent each night till daylight wondering what the attraction could be. I attempted to notate and report the activity. Our only company during these long surveillances were strange little coatimundi who found us to be quite the curiosity.

After several days, the NG boys had grown quite weary of the military rations and took a tremendous liking to my special recipe of *green chile* venison stew, which I painstakingly concocted over a mesquite fire in the Dutch oven. Great breakfasts of eggs and healthy portions of Laney sausage were savored at breakfast after long nights of observing the all-night vehicle traffic. There was talk among the NG boys about the foolish reluctance of the helicopter crew chief to pack my ice chest onto the Huey. After six days the provisions ran dry, but our interest was drawn to the incessant nighttime traffic at the remote little Mexican farm. Finally, the helicopter returned and hauled us back to town where hot showers were the first order upon arrival. Our reports of the suspicious activity were quickly dismissed as over-enthusiasm for the operation. We were then reminded that the activity was taking place in the Republic of Mexico, well out of our jurisdiction.

Ten days later I got a visit by a friend from the dusty little town of Las Palomas, Chihuahua. He was carrying a copy of the daily newspaper from Casas Grandes. On the front page was an article detailing a recent raid on a marijuana plantation by elements of the Mexican Federal Judicial Police. The plantation had been located on a remote farm on the border near the New Mexico boot heel. Thousands of pounds of marijuana had been seized. I was to later find out that the nighttime traffic had been that of the growers who had been shooting marijuana-eating deer out of the patch with AK-47s.

Sometime later I got a phone call from one of the NG boys requesting the *green chile* venison stew recipe. Along with the recipe, I gave him a rundown of what had taken place at the little Mexican farm and we both reminisced on the operation. Finally, after a bit of hesitation, he chuckled and said, "I bet their venison stew sure couldn't compare to ours."

G&A February 2000

CHAPTER 30

Big Bend's Murder Steer Incident

The bend of the Rio Grande River makes a southeasterly turn just upriver from the Chihuahuan village Pilares, and flows smoothly through the thick salt cedar and mesquite country toward Presidio, on to Lajitas and Boquillas del Carmen. There it snakes back northward through spectacular canyons before heading east again.

This huge crook in the great river's path—the Big Bend of Texas—is well over 400 miles long. The sheer vastness, ruggedness and beauty of the Big Bend is world-renowned. It cradles the Big Bend National Park, Big Bend Ranch State Park and countless cattle ranches that have been the lifeblood of the area for well over a century.

One of my favorite area hangouts is Big Bend Saddlery in Alpine, Texas. There's a steady flow of characters through the shop doors: ranchers, lawmen, all sorts of collectors and a few old desert rats. It's a good place to consort with the afore-mentioned, shop for cowboy gear, books, or just to enjoy the pungent smell of new leather.

Recently, fellow border lawman Bill Fort and I were loitering at Big Bend Saddlery when Joe Richardson ambled in. It didn't take too long for us to fall into conversation about antique guns.

"Joe, you still packin' around that murder steer rifle?" Bill asked. "Yeah, but I may have 'er sold to a lady from over near Brady," Joe said. He looked at me as if I knew what a "murder steer" rifle was. "I've been negotiating with the university museum, too, but we haven't reached a deal," he said.

We stood in a circle around a new Big Bend custom saddle, admiring it in silence. *What in tarnation is a murder steer rifle?* I thought to myself, too embarrassed to ask for fear of humiliation.

More prattle about the murder steer gun ensued, and at last I felt it best to shame myself by revealing my ignorance rather than to miss the entire point of the conversation. A rest in discourse came, during which much handling of the leather goods took place, and I finally gathered up some nerve. "What do you mean by 'murder steer'?" I asked.

Bill and Joe looked startled. The entire establishment seemed to fall silent and the clientele, employees and owner, Gary Dunshee, eyeballed me in disbelief. After a few moments, they slowly returned to what they were doing, still shaking their heads.

It was a famous and dark incident in Brewster County, Texas, history. Some say it was a result of range war among cattlemen. More likely, it was an ordinary incident, like those that occurred with great frequency in those wild days.

Early in 1891, cowboys from a number of surrounding outfits were gathering herds northeast of Alpine to cull and ship yearlings. They had all gathered to one point and were in the process of cutting out respective brands.

Minute details are varied, though the calamity of the incident is clear. There was an argument between a cowhand, Fine Gilliland, who worked for a big outfit, Dubios and Wentworth, and Henry Harrison Powe, a small rancher and Civil War veteran. The dispute was over a sole, unbranded, brindle steer which was without a mother cow. Powe

119

and several other men provided strong evidence that the steer belonged to them. Gilliland insisted there was no proof and the steer belonged to D&W.

After the initial trouble, Powe borrowed a pistol and started to drive the steer toward his herd. Gilliland tried to rope the steer, at which time Powe fired a shot at the steer—not to kill it, but to scare it away from Gilliland. Gilliland then pulled his own pistol, dismounted and shot and wounded Powe. More shots were exchanged and Gilliland, unharmed, finally killed Powe.

Gilliland then mounted his horse and departed, knowing there were numerous witnesses. The Texas Rangers were dispatched after Gilliland a short time later; Rangers Thalis Cook and James Putman were soon on his trail.

The two confronted Gilliland several days later and another gunfight ensued. Gilliland killed both their horses and shot Cook in the kneecap before fleeing on his own horse. Putman, his Winchester resting over the body of his dead horse, shot the departing Gilliland in the head.

After Gilliland's departure from the Powe murder scene, remaining cowhands, mortified by Powe's killing, roped and tied down the hapless brindle steer. With a heated running iron, the word "Murder" was branded across its side as a reminder of the foul incident which would not soon be forgotten.

Legend varies regarding the fate of the steer, though some say it wandered for years, exiled even by its own kind.

A day or so after I heard the tale, Joe Richardson ran me down. "Got some-thing to show ya," he said, pulling a rifle case from the back of his truck. It was a Winchester Model 1886 .45-70 in excellent condition with honest wear on the barrel and a good bit of original case hardening on the frame. The receiver was engraved: "James A. Putman, Company 'D,' Frontier Battalion, Texas Rangers."

Too bad Henry Harrison Powe, or the "Murder" steer, could not have known that such a fine gun redressed their sorrowful destinies.

G&A January 2002

CHAPTER 31

The damn things stink, son.

There's a distinct feeling you get in the evening stillness in the south Texas *brasada* country in early fall. The sounds of coyotes whooping it up in the distance, deer and javelina rooting around in the brush and cattle bawling at distant water holes occasionally break the stillness and add to the very special atmosphere.

It was on such an evening almost 30 years ago that I first appreciated that feeling. A slight chill was in the air as my dad and I sat under a mesquite tree near an opening in the thick brush where javelina were known to frequent at that time of day. I was packing my Savage 99 .243, and Dad had his ever-present Ruger flat-top .44, both of us anticipating a shot at one of the Shipp Ranch's wily javelina. Our good friend and host, Evan Quiros, had stayed back at the ranch headquarters preparing us a supper of tasty *cabrito asado*, kid goat roasted over hot mesquite coals. Since *cabrito* was one of my favorite dishes, my mind began to wander from javelina hunting to supper.

"Dad how come we never take javelina home and eat 'em?" I queried.

Dad sat puffing on an unfiltered Camel, intently looking at nothing. A coyote yipped in the distance and we both looked in his general direction.

"They're not fit to eat, boy" He finally replied "The meat smells just like they do—*bad*."

I had been javelina hunting many times before with Dad and Evan, and eating one had never really crossed my mind. But as I pondered the thought, it seemed reasonable that javelina meat should taste more or less like hog. But Dad and Evan had always seemed content simply testing out .44 bullets on them.

Shortly after dusk, having lost our shooting light, we headed down the rough dirt road that led back to the Shipp Ranch headquarters. No javelina had chosen to show themselves that evening, depriving Dad of the opportunity to test some new .44 bullets he had. As we sat down to our savory meal that night with Evan, I again mentioned my curiosity about the gustatory qualities of the collared peccary, partially in hopes that our host might disagree with Dad's highly negative opinion. It was not to be.

Evan also shook his head and said, "The damned things stink, son and the meat smells just like they do.

Evan went onto explain that occasionally the hired men from Mexico- who came for part-time cowhand work-made tamales out of javelina meat, but otherwise the stuff was absolutely inedible. I then recalled that once I had eaten at the cook shack with my friend Esteban who had worked at the Shipp Ranch for many years. The fare had been *Son-of-a-Gun* stew, concocted from parcels of an old sheep that had been around the place as long as Esteban had. The cowboys had all delighted over the stew, though I wasn't as happy with it. It occurred to me that if cowboys found javelina offensive, it must be bad.

My opinion of the digestibility of the javelina remained the same for many years thereafter. I continued to hunt them occasionally accompanied by those who initially believed that javelina tenderloin might be quite delectable cooked over a hot grill. But I quickly steered them straight.

Bart Skelton

Years later I was stationed in Silver City, New Mexico as a young State Police Officer. My Sergeant was Jim Hiltsey, an avid hunter and connoisseur of wild game. Jim and I became close friends though our opinions concerning edible meats differed greatly. Jim believed that javelina meat was some of the most delectable available. I disagreed profusely. Jim explained to me that it was the butchering process that most people didn't understand. He said that the pigs must be properly cleaned, beginning with the musk gland located in the small of the animal's back, which, he explained, must be thoroughly removed and not be allowed to contact the rest of the animal prior to processing. He said that gloves had to be worn and discarded when working with the gland or the meat would still be subject to contamination. Jim insisted that, when properly prepared, javelina was an absolute delicacy.

I opined that Sgt. Hiltsley would probably have been in hog heaven at the cook shack down on the Shipp Ranch the day the boys had feasted on the sheep stew. I asked the old Sarge about the correct method of preparing skunk for the grill, and Jim didn't take my ribbing lightly. He was sure that I too, would be hooked on javelina barbecue after trying his. Finally, wagers were conducted as New Mexico's javelina season was not far away.

Red Rock is an area west of Silver City near the Gila River, on the Arizona/New Mexico border. It is a rough region, very difficult to travel on foot or horseback, but supports a decent population of javelina. Jim hunted it hard and, as I knew he would, bagged a nice boar on the final day of the season. The barbecue was on.

Jim who is well known in the Silver City area for his cookout parties, didn't hesitate to throw one featuring his famous javelina barbecue. Numerous guests showed for the affair, including a mutual friend of ours, a gentleman recently retired from the New Mexico Game and Fish Department who was unaware of the nature of the main course. As Jim was serving up the first heaping plate of barbecue, I happened to ask the old warden if he was a fan of javelina meat and was treated to a familiar refrain.

"Hell, boy, the damned things stink and the meat smells just like they do."
But I later mustered up my courage and forced myself to try it. Like so many times before on assorted subjects, Jim had straightened me out concerning javelina.

I found myself going for seconds.

G&A March 2000

CHAPTER 32

Mesquite Roots'

The beautifully carved, floral-patterned belt and holster hung from around his waist as comfortably as if it were a sash from a terrycloth bathrobe. The rig—made by George Lawrence up in Oregon—showed signs of extensive wear and was darkened by numerous dousings in saddle soap. After all, it had snugly shrouded the Ruger flat-top .44 Magnum—Dad's favorite shooter—for years. He had carried the outfit almost daily during that time, resulting in a good bit of wear on both six-shooter and holster.

The midday sun was causing a faint perspiration to begin beading up in the leather bands of our felt Resistol hats. Even early fall in the border mesquite country produces warm temperatures and—as we worked to gather wood for a cookfire—it was becoming quite noticeable. Dad had explained the particulars of our wood-gathering chore in detail, specifically describing the size of the mesquite pieces he wanted—as well as the locations where they would likely be found.

"My Yankee friends back east never understand when I tell 'em we have to dig for our water and our firewood. They don't know much about the desert," Dad said.

I contemplated the statement awhile, not really understanding what he meant since I had never been back east and knew no other way but to dig for wood when a fire was needed.

"The root systems of these mesquite bushes are huge," Dad said, lighting a cigarette. "When they die, the roots stay preserved underground for a long time. Makes great firewood."

After wandering around the thickets a short while, Dad finally pointed out a mound of sandy dirt from which several small, dead limbs protruded. He then began kicking at the outgrowths with the toe of his boot, unearthing well-cured pieces of mesquite about the size of his arm. We gathered several armloads, packing them back to our temporary camp.

From the bed of his old pickup, Dad retrieved a shovel and looked around for a likely spot for his fire pit. In a clear area some 20 feet or so from the truck, he excavated a hole about 3 feet in diameter and about a foot and a half deep. He then sent me back into the mesquite thickets with instructions to retrieve another armload of dry branches, each about as big around as a lariat. These proved to be little easier to harvest than the larger ones that had to be kicked up from underground.

In typical fire-building custom, Dad began with the small stuff first, placing a thick layer of light, dry branches over a wadded-up paper sack in the bottom of the hole. He then set the sack afire and—as the smaller branches began burning— began to add larger ones. Finally he ended up with a neat, 2-foot stack of burning wood in the hole. The thick, aromatic smoke slowly curled through the maze of dense branches and into the air, whetting our appetites. In the end, the entire pile would burn down on top of itself, producing a pungent set of hot coals, ideal for cooking.

Dad then spread a large, canvas tarp on the ground, not far from the fire. From the pickup he retrieved an ice chest, a large wooden cutting board and a set of fine, leather saddlebags, all of which were placed on the tarp. Sitting on the ice chest, Dad began sifting through the contents of the saddlebags, finally producing a sheath knife with stag horn stocks, along with a whetstone. He ran his thumb along the knife's edge, checking its keenness. Not quite satisfied, he stroked the blade across the well-used stone several times before checking the edge again. He repeated the process several times until the edge finally seemed acceptable to him.

I was captivated by the saddlebags and their remaining contents. Taking notice of my curiosity, Dad smiled at me.

"Care to do a little shootin' before supper?" he asked.

I answered with a smile and a nod. Dad again took to searching the contents of the saddlebags, this time producing two boxes of .22 ammunition and a small gun rug. He unzipped the rug and removed a little Colt Woodsman .22 automatic. We spent a while peppering an array of cans, dirt clods and prickly pears with the tantalizingly accurate little Colt until we just about ran through our 100 rounds.

Afterwards, Dad started preparing supper. On the cutting board, he sliced onion, bell pepper and beefsteak into two inch squares. He then produced two long, steel skewers and lanced the steak, onion and pepper onto them—alternating each chunk carefully. He then doused the shish kebabs generously with his own concoction of dry rub—salt, pepper, ground red chile, cumin and garlic powder. Dad then arranged several previously selected, flat rocks on the edge of the coals, carefully placing the ends of the skewers on the rocks, with the main portions about 4 inches over the coals. As they sizzled, drippings fell into the coals, producing curls of mesquite smoke touched with additional flavor.

Finally, we savored our mesquite-cooked meal to the sounds of the desert at sundown. The only accompaniments to the meal were cold biscuits, baked the day before and hauled to our campsite in a paper sack. Dad washed his supper down with a cold Mexican beer. I drank cold water out of a half-gallon milk jug.

"What do you think the poor folks are doing this evening?" Dad asked, looking off into the evening, deep in thought.

Being nine years old, I had no idea what he was talking about.

G&A November 2000

Section V

CHAPTER 33

Bears worst nightmare- Ashley's BCA

The 350-mile trek from my place to the Penn Baggett Ranch in Ozona, Texas, is a long but pleasurable one. The route passes through some of the most desolate country in west Texas before entering the hill country where Baggett's lovely outfit is located. Penn's place is occupied by a healthy herd of whitetails and an exorbitant number of turkeys—generally the objects of the early December gatherings of Penn's compadres at the ranch.

In my view, the wildlife is a secondary reason for attending the gatherings. Not that I would pass up a good hunt, mind you, but I savor the opportunity to shoot and swap stories with the many characters likely to show up. The December gathering has been attended by several famous characters including *John Wootters, Gary Sitton, Jim Wilson, the late Bill Jordan, John Taffin and Hamilton Bowen,* to name a few. In the company of such men at the Baggett place, I've found it best to keep my mouth shut and listen, taking in and learning from the continuous flow of information concerning hunting, guns, shooting and the dynamics of life in general.

In addition to the company, there's always a fascinating array of guns and ammunition on hand, brought to the Baggett place for use by all in attendance. Penn's bunkhouse comes complete with a handy 50-yard range right out the front door. During mid-day breaks from various hunting expeditions, the range is put to good use in the testing of various new loads and new guns. As well as a successful rancher, outfitter, goat herder, chef, and wildlife conservationist, Penn is one of the most knowledgeable people I know when it comes to hand loading and ballistics. Shooting gets top priority at the Baggett ranch and one can always expect to do a lot of it during visits there.

Our most recent get-together was no different. Unfortunately, many of the regulars were unable to attend, but it was nonetheless a memorable experience. Upon my arrival at the bunkhouse, I was greeted by host Penn, Sheriff Jim Wilson and Ashley Emerson. After a bit of catching up, we ventured out with the intent of taking a few of Penn's whitetail does. The evening hunt was successful with Sheriff Wilson taking a nice doe with his Freedom Arms .44 Magnum.

The following morning was equally successful with Ashley taking another deer with yet another Freedom Arms gun, the new .41 Magnum (which, by the way, performed exceptionally well). It was a well-placed shot, but you'd expect no less from the designer of the Ashley Express sight, one of the most innovative combat pistol sights on the market today. It consists of a large, white dot front with a tritium center and a shallow-cut rear designed for quick target acquisition. I was some-what skeptical at first about the size of the front bead and said so.

Ashley disappeared for a bit, returning a short time later with a double-action revolver of intriguing dimensions. It was from the custom shop of Hamilton Bowen and was built on a Ruger Redhawk frame. It had been converted, in Hamilton's stylish fashion, into a 4-inch .500 Linebaugh. The gun had been fitted with Ashley Express sights and sported a lanyard swivel on the butt. The grips and workmanship, as you might expect, were immaculate.

"A bear's worst nightmare." Ashley said proudly as he handed me the gun. "The lanyard is there so you can string it around your neck while you're sleeping in bear country. That way you'll be able to find it fast in case you're attacked."

His 6-foot, 6-inch frame looming over me, Ashley then handed me five cartridges. Their sheer size and weight were somewhat unsettling. I examined them for the longest while, something inside of me issuing warning signals. I have fired .475 Linebaughs, .454 Casulls and other powerful loads before, but these seemed a mite, well, *chunky* for my tastes.

"These are some of my own loads— 430-grain cast bullets over 34 grains of H110. They're moving right at 1,200 feet per second." Ashley said. "But don't worry," he added comfortingly. They aren't *near* as hostile as my other load. Go ahead."

I nodded and turned towards our target, a pie plate-sized steel gong about 30 yards out. I loaded the chambers of the big .500, recalculating the figures Ashley had just rattled off to me: *Four-inch barrel, 430-grain bullet, 1,200 feet per second...*

I broke into a sweat.

"I like shootin' it straight double action instead of single." Ashley offered helpfully.

I don't remember now whether I fired two or three rounds, but I do know that any damage inflicted upon that steel plate that day by a .500 Magnum was not my doing. Ashley shook his head, cocked his hat back and glared. "I know the gun shoots better than that."

Ashley quickly took the revolver from me, situated it carefully in his left hand, took a solid stance and touched it off double action. I'm not sure how many he fired one-handed that way, but I can tell you that a 430 grain bullet hitting a steel plate at 1,200 feet per second makes one hell of a ring.

If I were you, I'd stay away from Ashley Emerson in bear country at night.

G&A April 2001

CHAPTER 34

Cap and Ball Fanatic

The first time I shot one I was irrefutably hooked. The whole process was intriguing to me, from the manufacture of the round balls, the loading sequence and the satisfying roar after touching the thing off, with the thick, pungent smoke wrapping up the event. At the age of fourteen I was a muzzle-loading fanatic.

My dad played a big role in getting me started, but my old brush-beating *compadre*, Mike Laney of Lake Valley, New Mexico, was really responsible for my forth-coming addiction. Mike had been a muzzle-loader for some time and had even taken a mountain lion on his ranch with a Ruger Old Army cap and ball revolver at the age of thirteen, a deed that not many grown men have accomplished. Mike caused my interest in black powder to peak and showed me the ins and outs.

Not long after my initiation into black powder shooting, my dad graciously procured us a beautiful pair of Thompson Center .50 caliber Hawkens, one percussion and the other a flint lock. For one reason or the other, I fancied the flint lock and after shooting it, never really cared much about cap and ball guns again. Something about the primitiveness of it fascinated me. I spent my spare time casting round, .50 caliber balls and sorting them (I found them more accurate than mini balls) by the hundreds. I used my dad's shooting range in the back yard, firing as many rounds as possible without having to clean the bore. I had the cleaning process down to a science and could have the rifle cleaned up and ready to shoot again in no time. I would shoot so much that after each session my face, hands and clothing were black with powder residue.

My dad became so tickled with my absorption into black powder shooting that he took me with him on a muzzle-loader deer hunt at the Bataan Lodge located in the Lincoln National Forest in southern New Mexico with an impressive group of shooters. The hunt was sponsored by the New Mexico Game and Fish Department and included several of their officers, among them *John Goodwin* and his dad, *Hosie*, a retired NMG&F warden. Hosie went along as cook and turned out to be the finest camp chef in the territory. The party also included *Ken Ramage*, Navy Arms President *Val Forgett* and the late *George C. Nonte*. I felt more than fortunate to be in such noted company and relished the opportunity to learn more about black powder guns from some of the foremost experts on the subject.

I was a little discouraged when virtually every member of our distinguished party condemned my use of the flintlock on the hunt. It was their general consensus that a knuckle-headed kid ought to be carrying a cap and ball for hunting instead of the more intractable flintlock. But my dad knew what he was doing when he allowed me to continue with the flint gun. He had seen me shoot it hundreds of times and knew that I was relatively competent with it.

Unfortunately, the hunting at the Bataan lodge area proved to be tough and the first two days were fruitless. We emptied our rifles at the end of each day at a large rock about two hundred yards above the camp. I took the time to discharge several shots each evening which gained the attention of several of the party members. Wagers ensued among my elders. My flintlock proved itself reliable and more accurate than the rest of the rifles, which were all of the cap and ball persuasion.

On the last evening of the hunt, Mr. Forgett sat admiring my Hawken flint gun and asked me if I had a pistol to go along with it. I replied that I did not. He nodded his head and handed the rifle back to me, looking rather serious.

"Every rifleman needs a good pistol to accompany his longarm." Mr. Forgett said.

We departed the Lincoln National Forest the following day after a great hunt with an exceptional group of characters, and even though no venison was harvested, a lifetime of stories were exchanged and appreciated. These days I realize how fortunate I was to be a part of such a remarkable group of men.

Upon our return home I quickly fell back into my old routine of black powder shooting after school and on weekends. One afternoon about two weeks after the Bataan hunt, I received a package in the mail. It was addressed to me from Val Forgett of Navy Arms. It was one of his company's .36 caliber flintlock pistols with beautiful walnut stock and brass barrel. I was thrilled. I fired the pistol so often that I later had to take it to Bob Sconce, owner of the Miniature Machine Company and have the frizzen re-hardened. The brass barreled single shot became one of my prized possessions.

A few years ago I was detailed to El Paso, Texas for temporary duty in my capacity as a federal officer. Upon my return home to southern New Mexico, I was saddened to find my rural home disheveled by burglars. I spent considerable time inventorying the place but surprisingly found very few of my belongings missing. Oddly, only the brass barreled flintlock from Val Forgett and one other cap and ball pistol were missing. The TV, guitars and other valuables were untouched.

I frequently think of my old brass barrel flintlock and what use its new owner must have for it. It's doubtful he can even load it. But that notion is ethereal. Just another part of life on the border.

Bart Skelton

Update:
Since this article was published, I had the opportunity to run into Mr. Forgett, in Las Vegas at the annual Shot Show and upon telling him the tale of my stolen cap and ball pistols, I was surprised to find in the mail, another gift, a .36 Flintlock pistol. My thanks for fond memories rekindled. Val J. Forgett passed away on November 25, 2001 at the age of 72 years old. A man, a friend that will be greatly missed.

G&A December 1999

CHAPTER 35

Cadillac Ranch

As hail of .45 caliber bullets zinged over the men's heads and ricocheted through the rocks on the rough mountainside they had just negotiated, it is doubtful that the poor fellows were considering the salty nature of the two brothers on whose land they were trespassing. It's probable that no one, outside of the few that knew the brothers well, could have conceived just how salty they really were.

The trespassers had negotiated weeks of hardship, walking through isolated desert with little water or food while attempting to avoid towns, trouble and officials of the U.S. Border Patrol. The encroachers were illegal aliens from Mexico. Except for the fact that they had crossed into the United States without legal documentation, they were generally honest men looking for jobs that most American laborers had no interest in. They took these jobs in order to sustain their families in Mexico where jobs that paid enough money to purchase beans and tortillas are virtually non- existent—unless one wished to accept position in the drug trade. The men had come to the U.S. for years to seek such work, as had their fathers before them.

They didn't expect to run across two crazy *gringo* brothers who had come to the wayward conclusions that illegal immigrants were transgressing the American way of life. The Mexicans had passed through the ranch on their route to northern cities many times before without trouble-but this time they figured it might be their last.

The two brothers had been born and raised on the place. It's location in the south-central New Mexico, near the Gila National Forest and about 70 miles north of the border, had been a sanctuary for them all of their lives. They lived in the home that had been built by their grandfather shortly after the turn of the 20th century. They resided there in the same manner as he had—no electricity, no running water. The only truly modern luxury the boys enjoyed was a 1970 Cadillac that was torn up from years of running the disheveled ranch roads. The Cadillac was regularly put to the test carrying the brothers on harrowing trips to Chihuahua City in search of female companionship. In Mexico, the boys falsely touted themselves as rich ranchers. The excursions proved fruitful, and at least one wife was brought back to the ranch as a result, though the marriage immediately turned into a disaster, since the boys' ranch headquarters were far worse than the new brides' previous living conditions, which had been grim enough.

Some speculate that the ensuing misery brought about by the bad marriage to the woman from Chihuahua may have been responsible for the boys' decision to take arms against the illegal immigrants. The boys had even hired some of these men over the years when cattle prices were up and they could afford to. It didn't matter that they knew some of the men personally. They had made up their minds to do something about the alien problem, even though it merely satisfied a personal vendetta.

The boys were initially well armed. The older brother packed a 1st generation Colt .45 Single Action with a 4 1/2-inch barrel and the younger one a Colt Trooper in .357 Magnum. But they decided they needed a good long gun since their long distance proficiency with handguns was lacking. An acquaintance of the boys had recently been trying to pawn off an old Marlin .30-.30 and there was great speculation that the rifle had been stolen from a neighboring ranch. The $250 price was right though. About a week later, the sheriff had shown up at the brothers place with the true owner of the rifle. The rifle was relinquished, but the old man who owned the gun refused to reimburse the brothers a dime, infuriating the boys, though it wasn't the old rancher's fault they bought stolen property.

The old timer lived just a few miles down the road from the brother's place. The boys knew that he received a social security check every two weeks and that was his main source of income. They were careful during their surveillance of the old man's mailbox, ensuring that no one was aware that they were sorting through the old timer's mail after the arrival of the rural postal carrier. When at last the government check arrived, the two gleefully placed a stick of dynamite in the box, lit it and drove away.

Two weeks later, the boys repeated the process, though two sticks were necessary since the old man had constructed a new mailbox out of half-inch steel. The two sticks completed the task nicely, though the mailbox was not thoroughly annihilated.

That would be a lesson to the old man. It would take the government months to replace the checks.

As the two brothers sat plinking with their revolvers at the small group of illegals who had barricaded themselves behind a massive granite rock, they became somber about the situation. "If'n you hadn't insisted on spending the last of our scratch on that stolen rifle, we woulda had enough to make a trip back down to Mexico." The older brother said aimlessly firing shots in the vicinity of the Mexicans. As quickly as their interest in shooting at illegal aliens had piqued, it was

Bart Skelton

lost. The brothers ambled back to their ranch headquarters, packed the Caddy and headed south anyway.

Illegal work-seekers from all over Mexico continued to stream through southern New Mexico on their quest, but a word travels fast down there. The brothers' ranch, which lay along one of the most popular paths for the aliens, was avoided for years. Not until a few years ago, when the younger brother shot the older in an argument was it safe for the illegals to take up their old path again. The boys were forced to sell the place to pay the doctor bills that piled up as a result of the shooting.

Thus another chapter in the peculiar episodes of the southwest was ended-at least for now.

G&A December 2000

CHAPTER 36

Arrow Head Huntin'

Many people who have lived in the area or traveled through it often find it truly an unsightly expanse of land. The summertime heat can reach unbearable levels, coupled with dreadful humidity. Area occupants frequently ponder hauling off and moving to the North Pole. As a youngster, these thoughts never occurred to me as I didn't know any better. The blazing heat didn't faze me, and I had never seen mountains, so the flat, mesquite thickets seemed OK to me. As a matter of fact, I was quite satisfied with the way things were in Webb County, Texas.

Probably the most significant factor behind my satisfaction with life around Laredo, Texas, the largest city in Webb County, was the fact that my Dad was well acquainted with Colonel Evan Quiros. Dad and I became common fixtures around Evan's place, the Shipp Ranch. Though the country in that part of Texas seems miserable, it is actually rich in wildlife. The deer population is tremendous-javelina, coyotes, cats and other animals thrive in the thick mesquite country. Cattle generally do well, though they become wild as deer as a result of living in the thick brush country without seeing humans or horses for extended periods. Rattlesnakes of generous size festoon the landscape.

My Dad and the Colonel loved to spend time together on the Shipp, mainly shooting .44 Magnums and swapping lies. The ranch was an outstanding place for my Dad to test guns, hunt, visit with the Colonel and other cronies and generally have a good time. Dad was never without his 7 1/2-inch Ruger Blackhawk .44 three screw, the Colonel preferring his old long -barreled Smith and Wesson Model 29. I was frequently lucky enough to be included in those activities, and they were times I will cherish forever.

One thing my Dad and I learned about that South Texas country was that it had been inundated with ancient Indian tribes. The Shipp was blanketed with ancient encampments, open areas in the brush country where Indians had actually resided. These areas were usually covered with flint chips, remnants of the manufacture of arrowhead or atl-atl points. My Dad became fascinated with the camps, especially after finding numerous beautifully made points. He studied up on the subject with the help of a few books on ancient Indian history and later became a bit more wrapped up in arrowhead hunting than he did with game hunting. This development was much to the chagrin of Colonel Quiros, who didn't seem to be too interested in the archeological background of the Shipp. The Colonel seemed much more attracted to passing his spare time working up new loads for any one of the firearms in his impressive accumulation.

This resulted in my Dad and I spending more time making arrowhead hunting excursion onto the ranch without the gracious company of Colonel Quiros.

"I'll be glad when you get all that crap picked up so we can get back to shootin," the Colonel told Dad.

Dad occasionally light-heartedly accused the Colonel of sending the ranch hands out to gather up all of the arrowheads they could find and bury them. My friend, old Esteban, who had worked at the Shipp for some years, would frequently tell me he knew the exact location of arrowheads, and, in fact, would take me to them. I was seldom able to pick them out, and Esteban, in a roundabout way, would always make sure I found them.

The artifact hunting continued for some time, though we always mixed in some shooting and/or hunting during the trips. During the seasons, deer, quail and javelina hunting took place, though the excursions always seemed to be planned and the area known to accommodate a large Indian camp. Dad was fond of hunting quail with a Colt Woodsman .22 auto, taking them with head shots. He would frequently overlook downed birds for his incessant concentration on the search for flint.

Like most fads, the arrowhead hunting excitement finally slowed down after a year or so, and one spring afternoon found us bouncing down a dusty *sendero* on the Shipp with Colonel Quiros at the wheel of his four-wheel-drive pickup, no doubt happy that shooting and general ranch carousing were back on the agenda. As usual, I was riding in the back, perched on the pickup's hunting rack. The truck suddenly came to a halt and I saw Colonel Quiros pointing down a brushy arroyo. A big rattle snake was making his way up one side toward the shade of a large mesquite. Dad exited the vehicle, drew his .44 from his fancy Lawrence belt and holster rig, took a quick aim and fired. It was one of the quickest shots I had ever seen—a perfect example of snap shooting that left the headless snake withering at the bottom of the arroyo.

Dad and I ambled over to the snake, a full 6-footer. Dad stared at it for a moment then kicked at it a bit. I thought he was just making sure it was dead, though its head was gone. Then Dad bent down and picked up one of the most beautiful points either of us had even seen. It had been laying underneath the dead snake. The point was of red colored flint, with a long, delicate thin shaft and one pronounced barb. The other barb had unfortunately been broken off. Dad held the point up towards Colonel Quiros and grinned.

The Colonel tipped his hat back and shook his head in disgust.

Bart Skelton

That beautiful point remains the centerpiece of the arrowhead collection my Dad and I gathered together, which is now proudly displayed in my living room. It's been a number of years since I've been back down to the Shipp, but I'm in hopes that I'll someday return—but it's doubtful that I'll be adding any more Shipp artifacts to my collection.

At least if the Colonel has anything to do with it.

G&A May 2000

CHAPTER 37

Mom's Purse Gun
Women are takin' over everythin'.

Sally Jim Skelton-World Champion Bull rider 1947 and Trick rider, seen here on Skokie

The New Mexico winter was beginning to set in and it was looking like it might be a tough one. The clouds hung low on the mountain peaks, heavy with ice particles. The air was still and a few white flakes were appearing. Our trip to the high country had been a dual purpose one; looking for cattle that may have been missed during the recent fall gathering and to do some shooting with my Ruger Blackhawk .44 flattop. I had been granted a couple of days off from my regular job and had decided to head to the mountains for a quick visit.

My friend had been a cowhand all of his life and had worked ranches throughout New Mexico. He had packed his first generation Colt for many years, even though .32-20 ammunition is pretty expensive for someone drawing cowboy wages.

"My cousin, Hunk, he used to have a .44 Mag. He told me it was the greatest cartridge ever was, but after shootin' yours, I believe I disagree. Just too much gun," he said as we ambled back to his old pickup. "I've killed a bunch of game with my old Colt and she don't kick near as bad."

His response wasn't uncommon. I've known many shooters who think the same way, though I know a few more who don't believe the .44 Magnum is quite big enough. The growing popularity of the .454 Casull has definitely cast a shadow on the .44's once powerful reputation, and the older cartridge no longer carries the designation of the most powerful cartridge in the world. But it's still a fine one.

I, too, am fond of the Freedom Arms .454 Casull, though I believe I would be more apt to pick a .44 Magnum revolver for an every day packing gun. My association with the .44 Magnum cartridge started in 1966, when Dad tasked himself with disproving the negative opinions of those criticizing the .44 Magnum. A few influential shooters and gun writers of the day had instigated a push to discredit the .44 Mag, stating that the cartridge was much too powerful to safely fire in a handgun and was too punishing for the average shooter. Dad, being an adamant fan of the big .44, went to bat for it.

Five rounds of .44 Magnum ammunition in a Ruger single-action revolver is an intimidating sight to a youngster—I can attest to that. As I recall, I didn't fire all five rounds, but shot enough for my dad to take pictures. It was a proud day for both of us. I shot without complaining and, predictably missed the coffee can we had set up about twenty feet away. The pictures were later published along with dad's story disputing the claims of those denouncing the big magnum.

As far as I know, those nay Sayers have remained silent ever since.

My relationship with the cartridge has remained special since that day. I am fortunate to own a couple of good .44 Mags, including Dad's old flattop Ruger and an outstanding Smith and Wesson Model 629 with custom stocks built by Bear Hug Grips. I've packed these guns faithfully for years and have cleanly taken game with both. I've observed a few good developments in the cartridge over the years and have seen some great new production .44 Magnum revolvers become available. Along with that, I've also seen some unlikely .44 Magnum shooters evolve.

Some years back, Ruger introduced its excellent Bisley Model revolvers. These single actions sport grip frame and hammer shapes that resemble those of the classic old Colt Bisleys. Dad was lucky enough to get his hands on one of the first Ruger Bisleys, a 7 1/2-inch .44 Mag. For reasons unknown to all but her, my mother, Sally, has always had an affinity for the Colt Bisley, and when the new Ruger Bisley Model arrived at the house, she took an immediate liking to it.

"I want this gun for my own." she advised Dad. Taken aback, since she had rarely shown a great deal of interest in new guns coming in and out of the house, Dad replied "What do you want with it?"

"I want it for my purse gun." she said after a short pause.

When his laughter died down, a good bit of pondering ensued as Dad tried to figure out how to quash what he considered just a whim on my mother's part. But she persisted, and at last a deal was struck—a deal that Dad figured was a sure way to keep her quiet. He posted a clean target on the 20-yard backstop behind the house, loaded the Bisley with five rounds of full house magnums and told my mother that if she could place all five rounds in the black, off- hand, the gun was hers.

I wasn't present for the firing, but I do know that there were five .44 caliber holes in the target on the backstop. Dad walked around shaking his head for days. Even though my mother doesn't really carry the big .44 around in her purse, she still keeps it at her bedside and I sure wouldn't want to be the one attempting an unwelcome entry into her place at night.

"You know my mother carries a big Ruger .44 Magnum like this one. Calls it her purse gun." I told my cowhand friend as we climbed into the pickup.

He took a large dip of Copenhagen and picked up my Ruger, studying it closely. He expectorated out the window and shook his head. "Women are takin' over everythin'."

G& A March 2000

CHAPTER 38

Bill Jordan

The first time I was awed by the presence of Bill Jordan, I was a small boy of six or seven years, and that occasion was no less inspiring than was the last time I saw him-not long before his final departure. Before meeting Bill for the first time, I had heard my father speak of him often, usually in a heroic context involving tales of incredible adventure and skillful gunplay. Seeing that giant of a man in person and actually having the opportunity to be around him from a young age was an extremely rewarding experience for me and one that will no doubt stay with me for the rest of my years.

Bill was an icon for shooters, particularly shooters who carry firearms for a living. His 30-year career as a U.S. Border Patrol agent and his escapades during that time gained him legendary status among law-enforcement officers of every type. Young military men idolized him for his experience as a Marine combat officer clearing out Japanese strongholds in the Pacific during World War II. After his retirement, Bill became an instructor at Camp Perry, keeping a fine tune on his rifle, shotgun and fast-draw skills while educating others in the same. Bill also developed a shooting exhibition that he performed publicly for years. His appearances were popular with the Diner's Club, the Knife and Fork Club and the Executive Club and led him to make several TV appearances. During these appearances, Bill performed astounding feats with a handgun that left audiences thoroughly impressed even if they were only causally interested in shooting.

Bart Skelton

Jordan's amazing speed with a six-gun will never be forgotten. One evening years ago during one of Bill's visits to our home, my dad provoked Bill into performing an informal fast-draw exhibition in the living room for our family and a couple of my school friends. We broke out an old *Don Hume* river belt and my dad's slicked-up Smith & Wesson Model 19. Complaining that he had not come prepared to perform his "dog and pony" show, Bill proceeded to astonish us. He placed a quarter on the back of his huge right hand as it lingered about six inches over the holstered revolver. In the blink of an eye he drew and dry fired the revolver, the quarter making a satisfying sound as it bounced around in the bottom of the holster.

After repeating this trick several times, Bill proceeded to demonstrate to us how easy it was to knock the quarter across the room with the muzzle of the revolver instead of allowing it to drop into the holster, starting from the very same position. As marvelous as these stunts were, I have never been more impressed than I was the first time I saw Jordan, disintegrate a saccharin tablet with a hipshot from his Model 19.

It was the same Model 19 that caused my dad a good bit of grief in his capacity as a U.S. Customs agent one night down on the Rio Grande near Laredo, Texas. Jordan had recently been down for a visit during which he had taken a shine to Dad's Model 19, which had a silky smooth action and a fine set of Roper walnut stocks. Upon his departure, Bill slipped Dad's revolver into his waistband and left his own Model 19 on the coffee table, stating "you can have yours back when mine's just like it, Skeet." A short time later, Dad was called to do some anti-smuggling work in the brush down on the river, grabbing Jordan's six-gun on the way out the door.

As such operations occasionally do, the situation turned ugly that night on the river. Dad and his *compañeros* ran into a group of fighters and shots were exchanged. The following day, I greeted my dad in the front yard as he returned home. He was exhausted, having stayed up all night as a result of the foray. As I got out of his car, he tossed me a white straw cowboy hat with a bullet hole through the top

152

of it, a souvenir I kept around for years. Very little was said about the hat at the time, but I later discovered that the previous owner of the hat had been taking shots at Dad and his fellow agents down on the river.

The night was pitch dark, but the white straw hat was shining like a diamond. Dad had lined his sights up in the center of the hat, then moved the muzzle down slightly in estimation of the center of the smugglers forehead. The bullet put a new crease in the *contrabandista's* brim but left him generally unharmed. You see, Jordan's gun was sighted just a few inches higher for dad's eyes- a phenomenon that he never let Bill live down.

The six-foot, six inch Louisiana gentleman had a way with words, both spoken and written, that will be sorely missed. Most people who had the good fortune of spending any time around Bill usually walked away from him in good humor as a result of some amusing anecdote he would spin. I recall querying Bill one time about one of his African safaris, particularly the dangers of stalking elephant. Bill replied in his slow Southern drawl, "Dem ain't the kind you feed peanuts to, Son."

Bill left us with years of magnificent stories through his monthly column and two exceptional books, *Mostly Huntin'* and *No Second Place Winner*. The latter is one of the finest and most fascinating books on combat shooting to date. He also left us with the realization that true heroes such as he are hard to find.

Adventurer, showman, scribe and always a gentleman, Bill Jordan was a true character the likes of which the shooting world will not likely see again. He was indisputably a fine man to have with you down on the border.

Editor's note: Bill Jordan died October 4, 1997, in Linden, Texas, as a result of heart disease. He was 86.

G&A March 1998

CHAPTER 39

South of the Border Single Actions

The Great Sonoran Desert is truly one of the wonders of North America. Encompassing the southern part of Arizona, it also makes up the Mexican state of Sonora. Scorching in the summertime and tolerable in the winter months, this region teems with an extraordinary variety of plants and wildlife. People who've never been there assume that it's barren and lifeless, but many of those same folks often don't want to leave after their first visit.

It was in that very desert that the life of many a fine Colt Single Action Army was resurrected. Mexico was a major recipient of American firearms around the turn of the last century. The Mexican Revolution accounted for the importation of a great number of American-made small arms. Colt, Winchester, Smith & Wesson and other manufacturers were responsible for these shipments, but I would guess that many of the arms found their way down there in a less-than-legitimate fashion.

Many a good Single Action Army and Bisley Model Colt fell into the hands of Mexicans who put them to hard—and often deadly—use. Single-action handguns and lever-action rifles were quite common in Mexico—especially along the border—until 40 or 50 years ago. Unfortunately, harsh and senseless gun laws put an end to gun ownership by law-abiding Mexican citizens. These days, only the rich, the police and drug dealers can get away with owning a firearm in Mexico.

Back in the mid-1950s, the scenario for gun owners and traders wasn't so grim in Mexican border country. Gringo gun traders were beginning to figure out that good guns could be had in Mexico for a fraction of the price they might bring in the States.

Two such enterprising types in particular dreamed up a scheme to pick up old Colt single actions that were being put to use as chili stirrers in Mexico and refurbish them to excellent condition.

When my Dad and *Kirk Barclay* first met, they knew they had a destiny south of the border. They both loved old Colt revolvers, both knew the border, and both were relatively fluent in Spanish. And their mutual interest in Mexican Revolutionary history—plus a familiarity with good tequilas—didn't hurt either.

Neither of them had an excess of funds with which to purchase guns, but they had good trading material: a few modern, inexpensive firearms in common calibers that would be more appealing to Mexican gun owners than antique chambering. Forty-five Long Colt, .44-40 and .32-20 ammunition was expensive and hard to come by in Mexico in those days. The traders also had a gift for getting acquainted with local police officers in Sonora who could point them in the direction of prospective clients.

After several trips into Sonora, Dad and Kirk found themselves with a commendable supply of Colts, S&W Schofields and a few Winchesters. The Smiths and Winchesters weren't at the top of their list, though. They both were continuously in search of the revered single-action Colts, and before it was all over, there were plenty of them in their respective collections.

Generally, the Colts were in quite rough condition when Dad and Kirk exported them back to the U.S. Upon returning home (at the time, it was O.K. to bring the guns back through Customs as American goods returned), they would rework the old hoglegs, usually replacing the barrels and cylinders if necessary, and doing other types of general rebuilding and refinishing. Occasionally, specimens bearing a good deal of original case hardening were found and left "as is," but they were rare.

The two traders seldom kept the Colts for themselves. The antiques were traded for more modern guns or sold to pay for the next adventure south. But there were exceptions.

Apparently, the trading got tougher as pawnshop men from Tucson, Phoenix and other big cities began catching on to the fact that bargains were to be had down south. Along with this, a problem emerged as the word went out in the small Sonoran towns about the two gringos packing valuable merchandise. Their descriptions became known and *banditos* became an issue. Trouble ensued, but the exact details were kept secret by the two traders, though I occasionally still hear old rumors about what may have happened during that last trading venture into Sonora.

Anyway, the adventures came to a halt. But two souvenirs were redeemed and are still around today. Dad and Kirk decided to commemorate their Mexican adventures by rebuilding a pair of Colt Single Action Army revolvers that they had ferreted out of a *pueblito* in Sonora. They converted the old six-guns—which had both started life as .44-40s—to .44 Specials and fitted them with 7-inch barrels. And they were able to come up with two sets of beautiful ivory stocks to finish the pair off with. They turned out to be a divine, matched pair of guns with a history that can only be imagined. Dad and Kirk took one each.

Years later, we moved to southern New Mexico, near the Mexican border, and happened to live just down the road from Kirk. Dad hadn't been in contact with Kirk for some time prior, but the two struck up their old friendship again. As it turned out, Kirk had been down on his luck and had sold his .44 to a local collector, Brian Armstrong, who sported an enviable collection. A few years later, Dad decided that the pair needed to be together and swapped his .44 to Mr. Armstrong for another collectible he needed for his own collection. The pair of Sonoran Colts have remained together since.

Some years have gone by now, and Kirk, Dad and Mr. Armstrong have all passed on. It is my understanding that much of the Armstrong collection has changed hands, but the pair of Sonoran .44s remain in the family—two pieces of history that should remain down on the border.

G&A August 2000

CHAPTER 40

Cuerno de chivo

It's been going on for many years now. I'm not sure exactly when it may have started, but I would guess that it was along about the time that *gringos* first migrated to the Mexican border. It's a certain feeling of curiosity that comes over a person standing on American soil, gazing over the expanse of the northern edge of Mexico. It's a sense of wonderment over a strange land in our own backyard where a different culture conducts itself in a different manner than ours.

It's the curiosity over that simpler lifestyle that draws Americans south across the border. For many, the journey into Mexican border towns is a pleasant one, filled with exotic sights, sounds and smells as they venture through shops and watering holes, bartering with the locals and spending money on various types of curios. The unfortunate aspect of this picture is the fact that most of those visitors rarely give much thought to the danger they might be in, even in places that may even be advertised as safe or popular with *turistas*.

It's true that most of those travelers safely return home to relate to their friends and families what a friendly, interesting place Mexico is. But that's not always the case. Sunday evenings bring out the citizenry in Mexico. It's the time when everyone socializes. Restaurants and *cantinas* are full, dances are held and people generally enjoy themselves.

It was such a Sunday a few years back that some friends of mine from southern New Mexico headed across the border into a small Chihuahuan community for an evening out. Their destination was a combination curio/furniture store that sported an adjoining restaurant and *cantina.* The establishment is well known for serving exceptionally good, garlic-marinated steaks. The clientele invariably consists of locals from both sides of the border, tourists and generally a few drug traffickers spending their proceeds.

This Sunday was no different, and as the evening wore on my friends enjoyed margaritas, thick steaks and music provided by an excellent mariachi band. As the couple finished their meal and were preparing to pay their tab, the festive mood of the establishment was disturbed somewhat by a commotion back in a dark corner.

Seated at the table in that corner were several of the town's renowned criminals—drug smugglers who had evaded the law on both sides for some time. They had apparently lost some of their caution that evening and were quite inebriated. A disagreement had broken out, allegedly over a girl but more than likely an unpaid drug debt.

The situation rapidly escalated from raised voices to raised fists then, finally, a raised knife. At that point the occupants of the table—along with most of the restaurant's customers—disbursed. My friends quickly made their way out the door to their car and back to the port of entry. They were lucky they did.

The would-be victims of the knifing also escaped out the front door of the restaurant, went straight to their parked vehicle to retrieve one of the most popular tools of the Mexican drug traffickers, a cuerno de chivo. The AK-47 is widely used by Mexican narco-traffickers, as well as various Mexican police agencies. In Mexico, it is referred to as the cuerno de chivo, or goat horn, due to its long, curved magazine.

Many traffickers wear gold amulets in the shape of the AK-47 around their necks or as decorations hanging from their rearview mirrors. The

Bart Skelton

most unfortunate aspect of this situation is the fact that the vast majority of Mexican citizens adhere to their country's severe gun laws, which virtually ban anyone from owning any type of firearm. In a place where drug lords rule, that amounts to a bad situation indeed.

The AK-47-wielding drug dealer rushed right back into the restaurant to settle up with the bearer of the knife, the last thing on his mind being the harsh penalties for the possession of his rifle.

A Mexican police friend of mine who had responded to the scene later told me that 80 to 90 rounds were fired. The fight progressed from inside the restaurant, to the bar and later into the street. Miraculously, only one injury resulted and it was relatively minor. The traffickers all got away with their hides and suffered no penalties from the law.

A week or so later, my old partner Miguel Briseño and I wandered down to the same restaurant for lunch. We had been well acquainted with the owner for some time, and upon our arrival we inquired as to his whereabouts. "He's in El Paso buying plaster and paint," said one of the waiters.

Miguel and I looked at him quizzically. The waiter then nonchalantly gestured towards the wall. Circular bullet marks had destroyed the outer layer of plaster on the south wall of the restaurant, also riddling a few of the old Revolution-era photographs that had adorned it. Miguel and I then noticed several elderly tourists having lunch— obviously guests from the RV park just across the border. No doubt they were down from Minnesota, Illinois or some other wintry state, enjoying the warm southwest. One of the gentlemen was wearing a large Mexican sombrero that he had just purchased at the curio shop.

Miguel and I watched as their attention shifted to the bullet marks on the wall. One of the ladies gushed: "They look so authentic."
Indeed they did.

G&A July 2000

Section VI

CHAPTER 41

Tommy Guns and Diamondbacks

"Gather yourself up there, boy, and come with me," Dad said, as he packed his camera, film, Ruger flat-top and a few rounds of ammo into his old hand-tooled leather bag. "Where are we going, Dad?" I asked. "Headed over to Snake Johnson's place. I need some good snake pictures for the magazine," he replied.

It was the late '60s, a period during which my dad had some difficulty juggling his incredibly time-consuming jobs as a federal agent and gun-writer, and occasionally trying to add in some family time, too. Weekends were frequently adventurous for me as Dad tried to combine father/son activities with chores associated with his writing.

Looking back on it, I suppose many of the things Dad exposed me to as a result of his job as a gun-writer might today be considered politically incorrect. Dad believed every boy should have a good .22 rifle and know how to handle a handgun. He started taking me hunting with him at a very early age and was disappointed that I had not killed my first deer by age 10. But after I shot a nice buck at age 12, he couldn't have been happier.

Shooting was an unequivocal part of Dad's life and he made damned sure it was part of mine. With a continuous array of test guns flowing through our house, I took for granted what many kids only daydreamed about.

"Does this one kick, Dad?" was a question he more than likely became sick of during my upbringing, though he would never say so. He offered me the opportunity to fire just about any gun he had, but only after careful instruction concerning its particular operation, loading and, above all, its safe handling.

One of the my most monumental shooting moments, came one weekend out at Colonel Quiros' place near Laredo, Texas, where we spent many of our weekends. Dad had recently acquired a beautiful 1921A Thompson submachine gun complete with fancy case, extra drum magazines and all the accessories. He was truly proud of it. I was captivated by it, as any young kid would be. Dad carefully pointed out the intricacies of the Thompson, teaching me how to change out the fore-end, remove the bolt for cleaning and how to load the drum, which I found difficult at first.

"Naw, it really doesn't kick too bad, but I believe you're a bit of a pup to be shootin' a Thompson, boy," he replied to my obvious question. He and the Colonel had been having a whale of a time shooting it, and I was more than a little jealous, especially since I was the one tasked with loading the magazines.

"Alright, Son, load that drum once more," Dad said as he stood there smartly, the butt of the Thompson resting on his thigh, muzzle up.

I did as he said and as I handed over the drum, I noticed he was smiling.

"Step on over here and see if you can hit that coffee can out there," he said.

He stood next to me, making sure I fit the magazine into the receiver the right way and made sure the safety was engaged. He then instructed me to pull the bolt back, explaining that the gun fired from an open bolt.

"Tuck the stock under your armpit and hold the pistol grip tightly in your left hand. Fire three-round bursts—don't try to shoot too many rounds at once."

It was probably one of the first times in my life I experienced the strong feeling of adrenaline; I was thrilled, and a little scared. I felt a little awkward not shouldering the gun as I would have a rifle. I have no recollection of ever actually hitting that coffee can. I was surprised that the gun didn't recoil nearly as much as I'd expected. I emptied the 50-round drum and wanted more.

"Out of .45 ammo, Son," Dad said as he patted me on the shoulder. "I'll let you shoot it again next time." The Thompson was one of my favorite guns that resided in our home during my upbringing. Dad later presented it to his friend William B. Ruger as a gift. But Dad had plenty more guns to introduce me to, and did so when he had the chance.

"Ol' Snake's quite a character," Dad said as we walked toward Snake Johnson's run-down shack on the outskirts of Laredo. "He's been bit by rattlers so many times he doesn't even seek medical help anymore if he gets struck."

Snake kept a pit chock full of rattlesnakes of every size and color behind his shack. Not only was it his hobby to collect them, he sold them to researchers and other collectors. Dad called on Johnson when he was in need of a good snake photograph in a hurry. We walked out to the pit—I wouldn't get near the edge. Dad and Snake stood peered down inside, Snake holding a long rod with a hook on the end. Dad motioned me to join them just as Snake stuck the rod into the pit. As Dad turned back around, Snake tossed a four-foot diamondback at his feet.

"Dammit, Snake!" Dad hollered as he jumped back, kicking at the coiled rattler and instinctively reaching for his six-shooter, which he'd left in the truck.

"Aww, he ain't gonna bite ya, Skeeter," Johnson chuckled. "Take them pictures quick before ya scare 'im."

Dad was none too happy when we left Snake's place and seemed a little pale. He didn't like snakes that close to him. As we pulled out, he pulled his old flask out from under the seat of the pickup and took a swig.

"This gunwritin' business is gettin' tougher all the time," he said.

G&A December 2001

CHAPTER 42

Reflectin' on Rangerin'

Retired Texas Ranger Joaquin Jackson's favorite usin' guns

"I never liked a damn fully automatic rifle much for police work," he said. "It's a hell of a lot better to have an accurate semi-auto or lever rifle. The only time I ever had any use for a full auto was when someone barricaded themselves in someplace. A machine gun'll damn sure get their attention and cause 'em to start moving around where you can get a clear shot."

It was good advice, even if it hadn't been coming from one of the most famous lawmen in Texas. He'd come by my place and drug me out for a cup of coffee, which we were enjoying in a little diner in Alpine, Texas.

Joaquin Jackson emits a presence that most cops, and most men in general, envy. His six foot five frame is imposing, and scared the hell out criminals all over the state of Texas for thirty five years. As one of the most well known Texas Rangers of modern times, Joaquin, now retired, has seen his share of crime and criminals since his early days as a Highway Patrolman.

"Bout the only full auto I ever saw I really liked was a damned Monitor," Joaquin said in his deep, Texas draw. "You, know, a cut-off

Browning Automatic Rifle. The one I was fooling around with belonged to Frank Hamer."

The fact that Joaquin had actually handled Frank Hamer's BAR was fascinating to me. I'd heard and read about the Hamer's fancy of the BAR for most of my life. Many old stories indicated that Hamer had been carrying the BAR during the bloody shootout with Bonnie and Clyde, but Joaquin says that's all guff, and that Hamer had actually had a Winchester Model 8 repeater.

"Hamer's son had actually sold that Monitor to some folks I knew from down in South Texas. About the time all that Brady stuff came about, they decided they'd better get rid of it, so they commissioned me to take care of it. I hauled it up to Waco to the Ranger museum. It's still there today."

Just the mention of the Brady Bill and other types of gun control causes a change in Joaquin's demeanor. As a member of the Board of Directors of the National Rifle Association, Joaquin is devoting a great deal of his time to the preservation of the second amendment, and making a concentrated effort to get young people interested in shooting and guns. Though he's out of the Rangers, Joaquin is a special deputy for Brewster County, Texas and holds private investigator credentials, and still carries a pistol on a daily basis.

When we got back into Joaquin's truck to head back to my place, he reminisced some about the side arms he had carried during his thirty five years with the Texas Department of Public safety. There were a passel of them, too.

"Settled on the Colt Combat Commander," Joaquin said. "I just liked the weight and feel of the damned thing. Had several of 'em."

Then he reached behind the seat of his truck and grabbed a pistol, handing over to me. It was a Kimber Pro Carry in .45 automatic. The gun was the four-inch model with aluminum frame, outfitted with a set of checkered laminate stocks out of the Kimber custom shop.

Bart Skelton

"'Ol Dwight Van Brundt up at Kimber sent me this pistol the other day," Joaquin said. "It's a real dandy. The best part about it is the damn thing shoots."

Joaquin went on to say that though he'd been fond of the lightweight Commander, he'd experienced problems with them locking up tight, and some accuracy problems, as well.

"If I ever had to do any precision shooting at any distance at all," Joaquin said, "I'd holster that Commander and get my Smith Model nineteen. I knew it'd shoot out to fifty yards. If you have something like a hostage situation, you don't take any chances with accuracy."

Standing outside the Joaquin's truck before his departure, we continued to examine the Kimber. Joaquin hefted the pistol several times, worked the slide and dry fired repeatedly. It was evident he was taken with the .45, and didn't want to put it back in it's gun rug.

"I just wish Kimber would have come out with this thing when I was still Rangerin'," Joaquin said, cigar hanging from the corner of his mouth. "This is what I'd a been carrying. It's the best of both worlds - accurate as my old Model 19, lightweight, and higher capacity than a wheel gun."

The twinkle in Joaquin's eye verified his statement. He was serious about it.

From the lawmen who carry them, and those of us who wish we could, *muchas gracias,* Kimber.

G&A Jan 03

168

CHAPTER 43

Bowen's "The Custom Revolver"

Custom pistol smith Hamilton Bowen describes everything there is to know about custom wheel guns in his new book except how to abuse them down in the brush country.

From the standpoint of technology, the things are ingenious, constructed by engineers possessing true infatuation with their craft. The effort and brainpower involved in their design and manufacture could only have been achieved by true artisans and virtual geniuses. The results of all this hard work have intrigued the masses for ages, and along with the captivation, they've provided protection, equalization, fascination and pure pleasure.

Revolving firearms have been around a long time. Experimental models, most relatively inept in performance, were developed sometime in the sixteenth century, and employed an advancing list of ignition devices including the wheel, match and flint lock, and later the percussion and cartridge models. Though not without competition, Samuel Colt developed the revolver into a booming success, revolutionizing the handgun and turning the tables for entities such as the Texas Navy and later the Texas Rangers, who utilized Colt's repeater design to even the score in battle. The further accomplishment and prosperity of Colt, Smith and Wesson and Ruger need no mention here.

Bart Skelton

If Samuel Colt was the true father of the revolving pistol, then Hamilton Bowen is his favorite son of modern day. Indeed Hamilton was born to produce revolvers that can achieve no higher level of perfection. His work results in the epitome of a fine revolver - a piece of mechanical art that succeeds in discharging a medley of fascinating goals.

Good fortune resulted in my introduction to Hamilton Bowen a number of years ago during a go at the annual Shootist's Holiday up in Colorado. Hamilton was kind enough then to permit me to handle several of his classy wheel guns, an experience that enlightened my perception of the modern revolver.

In particular, his Alpine revolver I took a special fancy to. For manufacture of the Alpine, Hamilton takes on the elaborate task of converting a Ruger Redhawk into a short, round-butt, five shot version offered in several interesting calibers, including .45 Colt and .50 Action Express, to name a few. The end product is one of the handiest, most accurate, finely tuned and tastefully finished handguns I've ever fired. Some time back, my good friend, Gary Sitton, also a big fan of the Alpine, was kind enough to loan me his, chambered in .45 Colt. I made good use of the opportunity and kept the gun for several months. My practice of hiding the gun during each of Gary's visits finally became irksome, and I was forced to relinquish it, though not before firing several hundred rounds of .45 Long Colt through it.

But the Alpine is one of many variations of custom revolvers Hamilton turns out. His work with Ruger double action and single actions, as well as Colt single actions is prodigious. His reproduction of the original Keith No. 5 revolver is breathtaking and each time I see one I begin searching the house for prospective pawn goods that might assist in financing one.

Some weeks ago I received a package from Hamilton. My excitement piqued as I thought he must have sent some obscure new revolver to try out. I wasn't too disappointed to discover it wasn't a gun, but a copy of his fine new book, suitably entitled "The Custom Revolver". I've been immersed in it since its appearance and I don't believe I've had the privilege of studying a more comprehensive and entertaining work relating to firearms.

The tastefully done hardback volume begins by outlining the "raw materials" involved in the production of custom revolvers, delineating the various double and single action revolvers Hamilton currently uses as a base for his work.

Bowen Classic Arms shares a portion of its custom gun production with several other fine firms, such as custom grip makers Roy Fishpaw, Paul Persinger and Dan Pursley, barrels from Douglas, Krieger and Shilen. For much of their finishing work, BCA uses Doug Turnbull's excellent firm, Turnbull Restorations, which specializes in an assortment of intriguing services, including excellent case hardening and bluing, all of which is given space in Hamilton's book.

Hamilton further purveys detailed, well-written accounts of tuning and accuracy, describing the exacting work involving the hand-fitting and mechanical blueprinting required in the production of his creations. The book continues with detailed explanation of rechambering and caliber conversions, as well as general styles in finishing the end products. Other practical advise from Hamilton includes shooting techniques, reloading, grips, and insight on a number of truly unusual calibers and configurations of revolvers.

Hamilton's smooth, articulate writing style communicates the substance in a manner which will both educate and charm the reader, a quality that is seldom found in most volumes that involve guns. In addition, the book includes an outstanding array of photographs, including illustrative black and white that accompany the text, and beautifully executed color plates that offer clear visual examples of Hamilton's work.

Certainly, for those interested in custom guns of any kind, this book is a prerequisite. But I don't believe Hamilton's tome will be limited to those interested in highly specialized handguns - but anyone with interest regarding the operation, improvement and artistic values of them - or in general, who just plain likes revolvers and shooting.

It's doubtful that most of us will ever be able to afford a Bowen fancy grade Keith No. 5, which is hand crafted utilizing the United States Patent Firearms Flat Top Target receiver, Colt and custom parts, carbona blue with nitred small parts, deluxe engraving and carved ivory stocks - the entire package hand fit and finished. But Hamilton's book has at least provided us with the fascinating insight of how such a masterpiece evolves, plus a vast array of other engaging topics concerning shooting.

Besides, if I ever were to come up with the down payment on the fancy Keith No. 5, I doubt Hamilton would build it for me anyhow. Certainly, he wouldn't want months or years worth of his labor riding around in a worn-out holster down in the border brush country.

He wouldn't consider the fancy No. 5 the inimitable brush gun - but I might.   G&A

CHAPTER 44

Friends and family

Dad

Skeeter about 1970 in Deming, New Mexico. Law Enforcement Agent,
Gun writer for *Shooting Times Magazine*

The Author

Bart Skelton in the New Mexico desert, relaxing at one of *Charlie Pirtle's* (Border Agent/Tracker retired) Chuckwagon feasts. 2001

Laney Ranch in Hillsboro, New Mexico

Charlie Pirtle (*retired Border agent and Tracker*), revered for his knowledge, skills, his friendship and guidance, aside the Author with wife Kim, September 11, 1999. Another great gathering of friends at the Laney Ranch.

Skeeter and Friends

Skeeter and Evan Quiros in the 1970's. Good friends that stood by each other, traveled together, hunted game and arrowheads, much to Evan's dismay, were an intricate part of the authors life, shaping and molding long before even he realized.

The last Cattle drive

Sally Jim's father was a cattle buyer during the early 1900's.
A picture from the last drive that he and his wife orchestrated in the
early 20's through the Panhandle of Texas.
(persons in background unknown, family archive)

Out on the Range

A cattle boss's chore didn't only consist of moving the cattle. The Authors grandfather had to make sure enough food and accessories were available for several weeks to make a long trail more accommodating.
(Family archive)

The Chuck Wagon

The history of the Chuck wagon and preparing meals for the cowpokes on the range was short lived in history, but the convenience of meals on wheels, never died for many ranchers. Like this one used in the Small cattle drive of the 20's, they are very much alive and well in the Southwest still today.

(Family archives)

the younger days

The Author, preparing himself for a bull ride. For years, the author roped, rode steers and rode bronc's. Traditions kept alive for many generations in his family. Needless to say, he's given it up for more leisurely rides these days, but still finds time to throw a few loops.

The infamous Mike Laney (L) with Bart about 1985. Showing off Colts that started their personal collections out on the Laney Ranch in Hillsboro, New Mexico. The place of good time gatherings, where history has been unveiled and caches revealed and friends get a chance to kick back and relax.

Jeff Unger (R) and Mike Laney, dear friends of the author and referred to often in writing through the years, posed here horsing around with some of Laney's antiques. Laney is an knowledgeable expert collector and rancher. It is regrettable that Jeff passed away a few years back and his humor and friendship is greatly missed.

Artists at Work

Sally Jim performing on Skoki. Sally Jim still resides in New Mexico, as an Artist and Educator in needlecraft canvas creation. Her "Saintly" works are continually sought after. Still actively involved with horses, "Bubba" is her ride of choice these days, as Skoki passed on years ago.

About the Author

Following a path much like his famous father, *Skeeter Skelton*, the author spent 5 years as a New Mexico State Policemen and 14 years as a Federal Criminal Investigator, his current occupatoin. Bart's cowboy way of storytelling and writing, depicts life on the border with all it's endless adventures and illustrates the harshness and beauty of the Southwest.

Share his sometimes strange and captivating encounters with outlaws, his inspirational visits and memories with heroes and just plain shenanigans with shady carousers. Stories that will make you laugh, or make you yarn for your lost or traded treasures, but all the while they will either entertain you or educate you.

A lesson in every story, but maybe not the way you'd think.

"Like father, like son: Bart and Skeeter Skelton, two of the most talented gun writers ever to pen a thought.
Guns & Ammo Magazine 500th addition. November 2001

I think Bart is leaving some footprint's of his own. Every time I think of what a Law Man "should be", I think of what Bart Skelton is and has always been....the finest!!! I know I'm very proud of Bart and I'm lucky enough to even call him my friend.

Matt Hilbun
Austin Armor Products